On ADMIRALTY SERVICE

Able Seaman 'Ginger' Graham keeping watch on the upper bridge of HMS Devonia, *in the North Sea, early in 1940.* (Leslie Rashleigh)

ON ADMIRALTY SERVICE

P&A CAMPBELL STEAMERS IN THE SECOND WORLD WAR

CHRIS COLLARD

*It is upon the Navy, under the Providence of God,
that the safety, honour and welfare of this realm
do chiefly attend.*

Preamble to the Articles of War, 1662,
King Charles II.

TEMPUS

First published 2003

PUBLISHED IN THE UNITED KINGDOM BY:
Tempus Publishing Ltd
The Mill, Brimscombe Port
Stroud, Gloucestershire GL5 2QG

PUBLISHED IN THE UNITED STATES OF AMERICA BY:
Tempus Publishing Inc.
2 Cumberland Street
Charleston, SC 29401

British Library Cataloguing in Publication Data.
A catalogue record for this book is available from the British Library.

ISBN 0 7524 2777 6

Typesetting and origination by Tempus Publishing.
Printed in Great Britain by Midway Colour Print, Wiltshire

CONTENTS

ACKNOWLEDGEMENTS

I wish to express my sincere thanks to the following institutions and individuals for their assistance in the preparation of this volume:

- The Public Records Office, Kew, Surrey – the repository of the Admiralty records.
- The Bristol Records Office – the repository of the records of P&A Campbell Ltd.
- The Imperial War Museum.
- The National Maritime Museum.
- The Naval Historical Branch of the Ministry of Defence.
- The Admiralty Library.
- The Guildhall Library.
- The Royal Commission on Historic Manuscripts.
- The Glasgow University Archives.
- The Welsh Industrial and Maritime Museum.
- The Cardiff Public Libraries.

The correspondence of the late Mr H.A. Allen and the late Mr E.R. Keen.

Former Signalman Leslie Rashleigh RNVR for his recollections and photographs taken aboard HMS *Devonia*.

Lt-Com. Anthony L. Hammond RN Retd for his reminiscences of life aboard HMS *Plinlimmon*.

Dr Donald Anderson; Mr George Arthur; Mr John Brown; Mr Richard Clammer; Miss Joan Collins; the late Mr Howard Davies; Mr Laurence Dunn; the late Mr Ernest Dumbleton; Mr Ron Gray; the late Mr Syd Gray; Mr Victor Gray; Mr Alfred Harvey; Mr Ken Jenkins; the late Mr Graham Langmuir; Mr L.T. Perrett-Jones; Mr Sydney Robinson; Mr Bill Shields; Mr Ron Sims; Mr Peter Southcombe; Mr Derek Spiers; Mr Alan Stevenson; Mr Leonard Stevenson; Mr Keith Thomas; the late Capt. L.G.A. Thomas; Miss Gwyneth White and Mr Will Widden, for their reminiscences, some extensive, some brief, but all highly significant in the piecing together of this historical 'jigsaw'.

My particular thanks, once again, must go to Mr George Owen, not only for his knowledge and expertise which have been readily at my disposal, but also for much practical help in the preparation of my manuscript.

The quotations at the chapter headings are, unless otherwise stated, from Winston Churchill.

Sources and Other Publications

The major sources of information on which this book is based are the Admiralty records deposited in the Public Records Office. The relevant classes are ADM1 and ADM116 – the main series of papers concerning the administration of naval affairs; ADM199 – papers dealing with the planning and execution of naval operations in the Second World War; ADM53 – ships' log books; ADM167 – Board of Admiralty Minutes and Memoranda; ADM208 – Admiralty Red Lists; ADM177 – Navy Lists (Confidential Edition); ADM182 – Admiralty Fleet Orders; ADM267 – Department of the Director of Naval Construction, Damage reports; MT59 – Ministry of War Transport Minutes and Correspondence.

Of the photographs reproduced in this volume, those of identified origin are credited accordingly. However, in many cases it has been impossible, despite exhaustive efforts and extensive enquiries, either to establish the exact identity of the photographers, or to trace their present whereabouts. I hope that this 'omnibus' acknowledgement will serve as an appreciation of all those people in recognition of their work and their valuable contributions to this history.

Other Titles by Chris Collard

Published by Tempus Publishing Ltd, The Mill, Brimscombe Port, Stroud, Gloucestershire, GL5 2QG:

White Funnels – The Story of Campbells Steamers 1946–1968.
P&A Campbell Pleasure Steamers 1887–1945.
P&A Campbell Steamers from 1946.
Bristol Channel Shipping – The Twilight Years.
Bristol Channel Shipping – Remembered.

In preparation: *P&A Campbell Steamers – 1919–1960.*

Published by Wheelhouse Books, 4 Ty Mawr Close, Rumney, Cardiff, CF3 3BU:

Special Excursions – The Story of Campbells Steamers 1919–1939.
A Dangerous Occupation – A Story of Paddle Minesweepers in the First World War.

THE WHITE FUNNEL FLEET
OF 1939

PS Ravenswood *(1891) approaching Birnbeck Pier, Weston-super-Mare, on Easter Monday 1929.* (H.G. Owen)

PS Westward Ho *(1894) passing Portishead on Whit Monday 17 May 1937.* (Edwin Keen)

PS Cambria *(1895) arriving at Minehead Pier, 1938/1939.* (H.G. Owen)

PS Britannia *(1896) at Hotwells Landing Stage, Bristol, in 1937.* (Chris Collard Collection)

PS Brighton Belle, *ex*-Lady Evelyn *(1900) arriving at Minehead Pier in 1938.* (Edwin Keen)

PS Brighton Queen, *ex*-Lady Moyra, *ex*-Gwalia *(1905), arriving at Eastbourne in 1933.* (W.A. Pelly)

PS Devonia *(1905) laid up at the Underfall Yard, Bristol, on Friday 11 September 1938.* (Edwin Keen)

PS Waverley, *ex-*Barry *(1907) arriving at Eastbourne in 1938.* (Chris Collard Collection)

PS Glen Avon *(1912) arriving at Birnbeck Pier, Weston-super-Mare in the 1930s.* (H.G. Owen)

PS Glen Usk *(1914) leaving Penarth for Cardiff on Saturday 27 May 1939.* (Edwin Keen)

PS Glen Gower *(1922) arriving at Brighton in 1936.* (H.G. Owen)

The final Swansea timetable of the 1939 season.

PROLOGUE

After the end of the Great War the ill-considered Treaty of Versailles imposed severe constraints, both financial and territorial, on Germany. The Allies' conditions of surrender were deeply resented by her people and provided a fertile breeding ground for the rise of the Nazi party during the 1920s and 1930s. For many of the German people the party, with its nationalistic ideals, represented the only way for the nation to regain its pride and identity.

However, under its tyrannical leader, Adolf Hitler, the country substantially re-armed, and reclaimed not only the land ceded to her neighbours under the terms of the peace treaty but, without compunction, gradually began to seize additional territory on the pretext of 'protection'.

By the late 1930s Europe was riven by political and military tension. Great Britain and France, anxious to avoid another full scale conflict, pursued their policies of appeasement culminating in the Munich Agreement of September 1938, when the British Prime Minister, Neville Chamberlain, after several meetings with Hitler, proclaimed 'Peace for our time'. Hitler's promises meant nothing and in the face of more and more German expansionism, the stage was set for the inevitable conflict.

During the 1920s and 1930s the paddle steamers of the White Funnel Fleet of P&A Campbell survived the difficult years of industrial unrest, the Depression, and many summers of bad weather, but were now faced with the spectre of impending hostilities for the second time in their history.

The 1939 season began under a cloud of uncertainty; the deteriorating European situation was a cause of great concern. Nevertheless, all but one of the steamers were in service. The exception was the *Devonia*. During the preceding years her high coal consumption had led to her seasons becoming shorter as time progressed and consideration had been given to laying her up for the whole of the summer of 1939. She was, however, towed to Avonmouth for dry-docking on Friday 14 July, fully painted, bunkered and prepared for sailing. The weather during the early part of the season was appalling, with wet and windy conditions prevailing until the end of July, when the *Devonia* would normally have entered service. The company therefore considered it prudent to leave her moored to buoys in Avonmouth Dock while the *Westward Ho* took her place at Swansea.

In company with the *Westward Ho* the Bristol Channel services were maintained by the *Britannia*, *Cambria*, *Glen Usk*, *Glen Avon*, *Ravenswood* and *Brighton Belle*, while the South Coast sailings were taken by the *Brighton Queen*, *Waverley* and *Glen Gower*.

The bad weather and low passenger figures pointed to a financially poor season; a particularly worrying factor in view of the large commitment undertaken by the company's ordering a new vessel in May 1939. This vessel, under construction at the Ailsa Shipbuilding Co.'s Yard at Troon, was to be a radical departure from the Campbell tradition. She was to be a turbine steamer, nearly 270ft in length and with a gross tonnage of over 1,700, destined to take over the company's continental sailings from the *Brighton Queen* during the summer of 1940.

During the 1930s two steamer enthusiasts, Mr H.A. Allen of Sussex and Mr Edwin Keen of Bristol, began a regular and prolific correspondence which was to continue for over thirty years. Both gentlemen were friendly with a number of P&A Campbell employees and therefore gained access to facts which were not generally communicated to the public. Their letters clearly reflect the spirit of the times and provide a rich source of information; although some of this information proved to be inaccurate as the course of events continually changed.

In several letters from Hove, dating from August 1939, Mr Allen stated:

The weather is now absolutely perfect. There are heavy loads on most trips and hundreds are being left behind on the Boulogne sailings – a regular feature during this fine August. Even on Tuesdays and Thursdays, when Eastbourne is the starting point for the cross-channel trips, the steamers fill to capacity, so the pursers reserve room for 100/150 from Hastings. An extra ship is badly needed between the end of July and mid-September, but the turbine will ease the pressure next year. [...]

I suggested to Mr J. B. MacDougall, the company's Brighton agent, that he would require a prolonged period of the present fine weather to make up for the nine weeks of stormy conditions which we experienced earlier in the summer. I was surprised when he told me that takings were already comfortably up.

'MacD' is annoyed about the idle Devonia which he says would have made a big profit this month if put on here to assist with the cross-channel traffic. It is a misfortune this fine ship has not been run. [...]

The Waverley and Brighton Queen are expected around here next season to run the coastal trips, but the Glen Gower will return to Bristol Channel service, probably from Swansea.

The turbine is expected to be cheaper to run than the Brighton Queen and will be able to carry about 1200 to France. She is to run to Dieppe as well as Boulogne and Calais.

The Brighton Queen leaves here for Bristol on 18 September, the Waverley on 25 September and the Glen Gower on 2 October, unless an emergency arises to send them home sooner.

I am still not expecting war to break out but the position appears to be very uncertain and delicate. Thousands of troops have already gone to France and hundreds of our bombers are now in France and Poland, so we are not likely to be caught off guard.

What a world we live in!

In the light of events which were soon to follow, Mr Allen's prophesies were to be proved incorrect.

CAMPBELL'S
REVISED SAILINGS

From Ilfracombe
(The Pier), and
Lynmouth
(Weather & Circumstances permitting)·

SUNDAY, SEPTEMBER 3rd.

Single Trip to Lynmouth, Minehead, Penarth, Cardiff, Clevedon and Bristol.
Leave Ilfracombe 5 p.m., Lynmouth 5-30.

Return Trip from Lynmouth to Ilfracombe.
Leave Lynmouth 1-55 p.m. Leave Ilfracombe 5 p.m. Return Fare 3/6.

MONDAY, SEPTEMBER 4th.

Afternoon Coasting Cruise along the N. Devon Coast to off Lynmouth. Fare 2/-.
Leave Ilfracombe 2-30 p.m. Due back about 4-30 p.m.

Single Trip to Lynmouth Minehead, Penarth, Cardiff, Clevedon and Bristol
Leave Ilfracombe 4-30 p.m., Lynmouth 5.

Return Trip from Lynmouth to Ilfracombe.
Leave Lynmouth 1-30 p.m. Leave Ilfracombe 4-30 p.m. Return Fare 3/6.

TUESDAY, SEPTEMBER 5th.

Single Trip to Lynmouth, Minehead, Penarth, Cardiff, Clevedon and Bristol
Leave Ilfracombe 4-30 p.m., Lynmouth 5.

Return Trip from Lynmouth to Ilfracombe.
Leave Lynmouth 1-55 p.m. Leave Ilfracombe 4-30 p.m. Return Fare 3/6.

WEDNESDAY, SEPTEMBER 6th.

Single Trip to Lynmouth, Minehead, Penarth, Cardiff, Clevedon and Bristol
Leave Ilfracombe 5 p.m., Lynmouth 5-30.

Return Trip from Lynmouth to Ilfracombe.
Leave Lynmouth 2-5 p.m. Leave Ilfracombe 5 p.m. Return Fare 3/6.

Note—All further Sailings are Cancelled.

SINGLE FARES from Ilfracombe or Lynmouth:

To Minehead 4/6, Penarth or Cardiff 5/6, Clevedon or Bristol 6/6.
Single Fare from Ilfracombe to Lynmouth or vice versa 3/-

For further particulars apply P. & A. CAMPBELL Ltd., 10 The Quay, Ilfracombe.

Telephone: Ilfracombe 158; Lynton 3114.

Chronicle Press, Ilfracombe.

*One of the revised timetables of Ilfracombe sailings which were printed late on Friday 1 September 1939.
By mid-morning on Sunday 3 September they had all been withdrawn from circulation.*

CALM BEFORE THE STORM

Astonishment was worldwide when Hitler's crashing onslaught upon Poland and the declarations of war upon Germany by Britain and France were followed only by a prolonged and oppressive pause.

The entries in the P&A Campbell memorandum book for Saturday 2 September 1939 are headed, 'Restricted services operational from this date'.

The rapid approach of the hostilities had led to the withdrawal from service of the *Ravenswood*, *Brighton Belle* and *Glen Avon*, which docked in the Floating Harbour, Bristol, later that day. The three South Coast steamers, the *Brighton Queen*, *Waverley* and *Glen Gower* were ordered to return to Bristol; all their further sailings having been cancelled. They left Newhaven, without passengers, on Saturday 2 September in convoy; the *Brighton Queen* at 09.20, the *Glen Gower* at 09.35, and the *Waverley* at 09.40. Just after midday they were stopped by an examination vessel already in position in St Helens Roads, to the north-east of the Isle of Wight, then proceeded south of the island and along the coast. They passed Start Point at about 20.00 and were abeam of The Lizard at midnight.

Great Britain declared war against Germany at 11.00 on Sunday 3 September 1939. At exactly the same time, the *Westward Ho*, having left Swansea for Bristol at 05.46, berthed at the Mardyke Wharf at the end of her curtailed season.

Mr Peter Southcombe, a former employee of P&A Campbell, was a schoolboy living in Ilfracombe at the time and recalls his experiences of that fateful Sunday:

I spent all day on the pier and heard Mr Chamberlain's famous announcement, '...this country is at war with Germany...', through a loudspeaker which had been rigged on the deck of the Brighton Queen. *She had arrived from Newhaven at 08.12 and sailed at 16.02, with seven passengers, direct for Bristol. The* Waverley *had arrived at 08.42 and sailed at 12.50, without passengers, for Bristol. The Glen Gower passed Ilfracombe at 08.15 but, not requiring to replenish her water tanks, did not call but continued to Walton Bay to await the tide in the River Avon. All three ships were required to stop by the examination vessel in Barry Roads, and berthed in Bristol at about 20.30 that evening.*

When the Waverley *sailed, her master, Captain Fred 'Ginger' Smyth, broke one of the brand new 'defence regulations' which had come into force that day – and made a proper meal of it! Hooters were forbidden, even for ships in port, except when used for emergency or normal signal purposes, and were banned altogether for factories, in case of being mistaken for air raid warnings. But as Ilfracombe was Capt. Smyth's home town and all his family and friends were there, he really enjoyed himself. The* Waverley's *hooter must have been heard for miles around and kept going for a long time with intermittent blasts. The* Brighton Queen *did her best to reply but at the time did not have enough steam to make much noise.*

Apart from the Cardiff to Weston sailings, only one trip took place on Sunday 3 September, when the *Britannia* ran from Bristol to Clevedon, Cardiff, Penarth, Minehead, Lynmouth and Ilfracombe. As her passengers enjoyed the sunshine and the scenery of the North Devon coast on the outward journey, the radio broadcast, at 11.15, in which the Prime Minister announced the declaration of war, was relayed over the loudspeakers.

Peter Southcombe's recollections continue:

> *A revised timetable for the Ilfracombe sailings had been printed late on Friday 1 September and was on all of the Campbell advertising boards throughout Ilfracombe and the surrounding area by Saturday lunchtime. By mid-morning on the Sunday the word 'cancelled' had been written in red across all of them. The Chronicle Press at Ilfracombe used to move very quickly when the Ilfracombe agent, Mr Fred Birmingham, wanted something printed. So did the bill posters.*
>
> *Fred was on the pier on Sunday afternoon and I remember his last words to the officers of the* Britannia *as she sailed for Bristol at 17.03 with 305 passengers – 'See you in 1943' he called across the water. There was little more gaiety and laughter aboard the* Britannia *that day, and it was a sad and quiet ship which docked at Bristol that night.*

From Monday 4 September all trips were cancelled except the Cardiff to Weston ferry, which was maintained for the time being by the *Glen Usk* and *Cambria*. The latter, however, ceased sailing on Thursday 7 September but remained in reserve at the Pier Head, Cardiff. A note in the memorandum book states: 'Cambria at Cardiff, on stand-by. Awaiting orders for evacuation of Americans from Weston.' In the event her services were not required and she lay idle for the following week.

A few days after war had been declared Mr Allen wrote to Mr Keen:

> *What a shame Campbells could not finish their season. They were well up on last year and as the weather has been fine and sunny since early August, they would have had the satisfaction of a really good season after all, the bad weather up to the end of July being more than compensated for later.*
>
> *I believe the* Glen Usk *is still working on the ferry on a restricted basis, but otherwise the rest of the ships are laid up in Bristol.*
>
> *It is very difficult to ascertain exactly what is happening these days and we can only hope that this blessed war will be one of short duration. [...]*
>
> *I expect work will go ahead on Campbells turbine as the Royal Navy has plenty of work for ships of this type.*

By Thursday 14 September ten of the eleven White Funnel steamers had been requisitioned by the Admiralty, the exception being the *Ravenswood* which had re-entered service, under the command of Capt. W.F. Watson, to take over the ferry from the *Glen Usk* on Friday 15th. On that day the *Cambria* docked at Bristol, followed by the *Glen Usk* on the morning of Saturday 16th. The ferry service, however, ceased altogether at the end of sailings on Sunday 17th and the *Ravenswood* left Cardiff for Bristol on the following morning. On Tuesday 19th she was requisitioned but the order was rescinded later in the day and she remained laid up at Bristol.

Naval Strategy

The immediate role of the Royal Navy was made clear by the First Sea Lord, Admiral Sir Dudley Pound, and First Lord of the Admiralty, Winston Churchill. It was to contain the enemy forces and keep the seas open for the passage of British ships. To this end a blockade of Germany was enforced similar to that of the previous conflict. Meanwhile, the transport of the British Expeditionary Force to France had been set in motion and was proceeding satisfactorily, with many of the country's larger excursion vessels and ferries acting as troopships.

The country waited but, on land and in the air, little happened. A prolonged and ominous calm prevailed; a phase which Prime Minister Neville Chamberlain termed the 'Twilight War'. At sea, however, the menace of mines and U-boats began slowly but surely. Nevertheless, the plans already laid by the Admiralty for the increased production of anti-submarine vessels were put into operation immediately and the convoy system, so successful in the First World War, was instituted straight away.

As far as minesweeping operations were concerned, every available Royal Naval minesweeper was at her war station by the end of August 1939. In addition trawlers and paddle steamers were once again requisitioned to strengthen the regular forces.

The paddlers were initially divided into six flotillas of five vessels each: the 7th Flotilla, based at Granton on the Firth of Forth, the 8th based at North Shields on the Tyne, the 9th at Harwich, the 11th at Greenock, and the 10th and 12th at Dover. This preliminary formation of the flotillas was, however, changed as the war progressed and as circumstances demanded.

The ships were manned, as before, mainly by personnel of the Royal Naval Reserve and Royal Naval Volunteer Reserve, many of whom formed an invaluable nucleus of officers and ratings who returned to the service with practical knowledge of minesweeping gained in the previous conflict.

The Minesweeping Division at the Admiralty once again became responsible for all vessels and material. The Director and his staff collated and disseminated intelligence regarding enemy mine-laying, gave advice on tactical counter-action, and charted the searched channels through which shipping might safely pass – the fairway known as the 'War Channel'. In the operations room a permanent watch plotted the movements of the sweepers, recorded the position of every mine that the enemy was known to have laid, and of every ship known to have been mined.

At each naval base a Port Minesweeping Officer took command of the vessels which swept the War Channel. As soon as a mine had been reported or swept, its position was buoyed, the local traffic was diverted and, if necessary, nearby ports were temporarily closed. If mines were found in the War Channel, the convoys were held back until the danger area had been cleared; a priority message would then be sent to the Minesweeping Division, where its information would be checked before being broadcast to all shore stations and ships at sea. Patrol vessels were also posted near the danger area to warn all ships which might not have received the message.

Refinements

An improved method of minesweeping had evolved since the First World War. The Oropesa sweeping apparatus, named after the trawler *Oropesa*, which had first used it in 1919, consisted of a pair of torpedo-shaped floats which were towed behind the vessel at the end of long sweep wires. Each wire was submerged by a 'kite' positioned close to her stern. The design of the kite had changed since the First World War; the new device helped to prevent entanglement of the wire and was much less 'temperamental' than its predecessor. Near the float was an 'otter', similar in design to the kite, which maintained a curve in the wire and held it at the correct depth. The mooring cable of the mine was severed by the sweep-wire which was usually fitted with cutters and a small explosive charge. Once on the surface the mine was destroyed by gunfire.

During September and October 1939 several merchant ships had been sunk at the entrances to various harbours, even though these had been carefully swept; it was suspected that magnetic mines had been responsible. Such weapons were no surprise, in fact they were a British invention and had been used off the Belgian coast in the latter stages of the Great War. The magnetic mine was so called, not because it was attracted to a ship's hull, but because it was detonated by a magnetic needle which became active when the ship's hull passed into its field. The mines were laid on the seabed and could only operate in comparatively shallow water, but within their range they caused far more damage than the contact mines. The latter would blow a hole in a ship, usually forward, which would be localised, whereas the explosion from a ground mine would strike the vessel under her bottom amidships, opening up the plating of the hull, shattering machinery and frequently breaking her back.

What was not known about the German magnetic mines was their polarity – whether they worked in the vertical or horizontal magnetic field set up by the metal-hulled ships. But good fortune came Great Britain's way when a German aircraft accidentally dropped a number of magnetic mines too close to the shoreline at Shoeburyness, in the Thames estuary, on 22 November 1939. As the tide ebbed one of them was recovered from the mud. It was dismantled and investigated by a team from HMS *Vernon*, the naval establishment for the development of underwater weapons at Portsmouth, and revealed the secret of its polarity. It was then a simple matter to neutralise the magnetism of a ship's hull by passing an electrical current through cables placed around the hull. In the case of smaller vessels, such as the paddle steamers, which were unable to generate a continuous electrical source of sufficient power for the purpose, experiments soon indicated that the 'wiping' of an electrical current around the hull from an external source afforded effective protection for up to about six months. The system was known as 'degaussing', after Carl Frederick Gauss (1777-1855), the German mathematician responsible for the discovery of many of the properties of electro-magnetism.

It was one thing to make the ships immune to the magnetic mine, but quite another to sweep it up or explode it harmlessly on the seabed. Eventually a method was devised whereby minesweepers towed two electric cables on the surface, one of 750 yards, the other 175 yards, and passed an electrical current down them which produced a magnetic field of sufficient strength to explode the mines. With the minesweepers working in pairs a wide area could be swept quickly and efficiently.

Fitting Out

The conversion of the White Funnel steamers for minesweeping began within a week of their being requisitioned. Their movements during September 1939 are summarised by quoting from the memorandum book:

Tuesday 12 September
Devonia. *Left Avonmouth for Bristol. Docked in Cumberland Basin at 18.25.*

Sunday 17 September
Brighton Belle. *(Capt. Findlay Brander). To Cumberland Basin at 07.45. Left at 09.35 for Penarth Dock. All officers put ashore after arrival. Penarth Pontoon Co. doing alterations.*
Glen Gower. *(Capt. William Riddell). To basin at 08.15. Left at 09.40 for Cardiff. Mountstuart Dry Dock Co. doing alterations who requested Chief Engineer, Mr Fred Hughes, to remain aboard until ship is completed, to advise them on various matters.*

Monday 18 September
Glen Usk. *(Capt. Bernard Hawken). Left basin at 10.00 for Penarth Dock. Penarth Pontoon Co. doing alterations.*

Tuesday 19 September
Devonia. *(Capt. George Spong). Left basin at 11.56 for Milford Haven.*
Brighton Queen. *(Capt. William Watson). Left basin at midnight for Milford Haven.*

Wednesday 20 September
Waverley *(Capt. Fred Smyth)* and Glen Avon *(Capt. William Riddell). Left basin for Milford Haven.*
Brighton Queen *arrived and reported at Milford Haven at 14.05.*
Devonia *anchored off Milford Haven. Docking at 11.00 on Thursday.*

Thursday 21 September
Glen Avon *and* Waverley *off Milford Haven.*
Later in the day Peter Hancock & Co. telephoned – all four steamers now docked in Milford Haven.

The remaining three requisitioned steamers, *Britannia*, *Cambria* and *Westward Ho*, were refitted at Bristol by Charles Hill & Sons Ltd.
  A letter written by Mr Allen in mid-September states:

On Wednesday 13 September all requisitioned White Funnel steamers were ordered to be in steam. Grey paint was being applied to the Britannia *and the after portion of her top saloon was being cut off between the third and fourth portholes from aft. The* Cambria *and* Westward Ho *were being similarly treated.* [...]

The wheelhouses being built on their open bridges are made of deal or pitch pine; they were made of teak in the last war. [...]

It is reported that the naval 'Brasshats' at Milford Haven say the war will be over by Christmas. If so, I shall be very thankful, but I hope it will not mean another one in a couple of years' time. [...]

It seems to me that some of our steamers will not be of much use for passenger work if and when they come back. At first the work of conversion went on all through the nights but all overtime was afterwards stopped. All the steamers have extra bunkers, below forward, where the officers cabins were. [...]

The Eastbourne agent, Mr W. A. Pelly, informs me that none of the captains have been taken over with the ships, although the engineers are absorbed. [...]

However, the Westward Ho's *peacetime skipper, Horace Rumsam, now Lieutenant RNR., has gone with her but he has a Commander RN. over him who was in paddlers in the last war.* [...]

The commander referred to by Mr Allen was Arthur L. Sanders RN Retd. It was he who, as a young lieutenant, seeing the Campbell fleet assembled in Bristol at the end of their curtailed season in August 1914, became one of the prime movers behind the requisitioning of paddle steamers for minesweeping purposes.

Mr Allen's letter continues:

The Royal Naval man who commanded the Glen Avon *last time, J. Collis-Bird, wrote to Campbells saying that he would take her again, and asked if Mr Thompson, who was his Chief Engineer, is still there as he would like to take him again. Thompson is still there of course, but isn't having any this time; he is getting on for 70! Several of the older engineers have taken shore jobs and there seems to be a shortage of men with paddle experience.* [...]

All of Campbells' wireless pursers are at the Filton Aeroplane Works, Bristol, assembling radio parts for planes. [...]

Let us hope it will not be long before the steamers have their white funnels again!

While the work of conversion was in progress the ten steamers were allocated to their respective flotillas, several of them undergoing a change of name to avoid confusion with other vessels. The *Brighton Queen, Devonia, Westward Ho, Cambria* (renamed *Plinlimmon*) and *Britannia* (renamed *Skiddaw*) were to form part of the 7th Minesweeping Flotilla. They were to come under Rosyth Command but were to be based at Granton. The flotilla leader, the *Westward Ho*, built in 1894, had the distinction of being the oldest serving vessel in the Royal Navy at that time.

The *Glen Gower, Glen Avon, Glen Usk, Brighton Belle* and *Waverley* (renamed *Snaefell*) were allocated to the North Shields command, where they were to form part of the 8th Minesweeping Flotilla.

Northward Bound

The *Westward Ho* was the first of the fleet to be refitted and began her trials for the Admiralty on Thursday 26 October 1939. A week later she made her way to Swansea, where she docked on Thursday 2 November, and by the end of the month had been joined by the *Plinlimmon* and *Skiddaw*. The three steamers were engaged on patrolling duties along the Gower coast until mid-December, when they left the Bristol Channel for the River Tyne, where they were to be based for about a month.

HMS Westward Ho *entering the Cumberland Basin from the Bristol City Docks on Wednesday 25 October 1939. She left the basin at 17.10 that day and spent the night at the South Pier, Avonmouth, from where, on the following morning, she steamed down the Bristol Channel on trials for the Admiralty. She returned to Bristol that evening and spent several days in Hill's dry dock before taking up her initial station at Swansea on Thursday 2 November 1939.* (Chris Collard Collection)

HMS Skiddaw *about to leave the Cumberland Basin for Avonmouth on Friday 24 November 1939. She ran her Admiralty trials off Barry on the following day and then returned to Avonmouth. After leaving Avonmouth, on the morning of Sunday 26 November, a severe gale forced her to shelter in Penarth Roads before continuing her journey to Swansea on Monday 27 November.* (Chris Collard Collection)

HMS Plinlimmon *(right) in the South Dock, Swansea, on Sunday 19 November 1939. Her trials had taken place on Friday 3 November, after which she had returned to Bristol for further maintenance, before arriving in Swansea on Thursday 9 November.* (H.G. Owen)

Above and below: *HMS* Westward Ho *alongside HMS* Plinlimmon *in the South Dock, Swansea, on Sunday 19 November 1939.* (H.G. Owen)

The *Brighton Belle*, *Glen Usk*, *Glen Gower* and *Snaefell* had satisfactorily completed their trials by mid-December. The *Glen Avon*, however, had left Milford Haven on Wednesday 6 December to return to Bristol for a variety of repairs to be carried out at Hill's Yard.

The trials of all of the steamers followed a similar procedure. As an example the log book of the *Snaefell* is quoted:

> 12 November 1939.
> *Ship commissioned at Milford Haven.* [...]
>
> 26 November 1939.
> *Shifted to coal tip and back to Fisheries berth after coaling.*
>
> 2 December 1939.
> *08.55. In locks. Proceeded to buoy to take on ammunition.*
>
> 3 December 1939.
> *Compass adjusting.*
>
> 6 December 1939.
> *Gun trials off Pembrokeshire coast.*
> *18.30. Moored at Ilfracombe pier.*
>
> 7 December 1939.
> *11.30. Dep. Ilfracombe pier.*
> *15.00. Docked at Barry.*

The *Snaefell* was the only member of the fleet to visit Ilfracombe after requisitioning. No doubt Capt. Smyth wanted to pay a farewell visit to his home town. Peter Southcombe recalls:

> *We did not know, when the* Waverley *made her noisy departure from Ilfracombe on the day war broke out, that she would be back. But there she was one morning, warship grey and renamed* Snaefell. *I could not get out of school to see her but knew she was at the pier, having been told by pals who had come on the school bus from Combe Martin. When I reached the harbour at lunchtime she had gone.*

The act of commissioning a ship into the Royal Navy is rich with history. The ceremony, however, varies according to the status of the ship in the Fleet. In the case of the wartime-hired paddle steamers, while the Admiralty did not deny the vital importance of their duties, the cermony was minimal.

Essentially a ship was in commission when an officer appointed to that ship arrived on board and gave the order to hoist the white commissioning pendant and the white ensign. The ship's books would then be opened for the entry of the details of her officers and crew.

This procedure, as short and simple as it was, changed the character and purpose of the excursion steamers completely. No greater contrast could be imagined than the transition they experienced between peace and war.

HMS Devonia *at Milford Haven. December 1939.* (Chris Collard Collection)

HMS Devonia *at Milford Haven on Saturday 2 December 1939.* (Leslie Speller)

HMS Brighton Queen *in dry dock at Milford Haven, Saturday 2 December 1939. The painting of her hull has been completed and the dry dock is being flooded prior to her departure for trials.* (Leslie Speller)

Above and right: *HMS* Snaefell *leaving the Fisheries berth, Milford Haven, to take on ammunition for gun trials. Saturday 2 December 1939.* (Leslie Speller)

Above and below: *HMS* Glen Avon *leaving Milford Haven on Saturday 2 December 1939. She sailed eastward along the coast of Pembrokeshire to the vicinity of the Stack Rocks for compass adjusting and gun trials.* (Leslie Speller)

At 09.00 on Saturday 9 December 1939 four ships of the 8th Minesweeping Flotilla assembled off Barry, where the *Glen Gower*, under Lt-Com. M.A. Biddulph, the Flotilla Commander, took station ahead, followed by the *Snaefell*, *Glen Usk* and *Brighton Belle* for the first part of their journey to the Tyne. At 13.55, in Bideford Bay, in a rising easterly wind and sea, the *Glen Gower* turned back to rendezvous with the *Brighton Belle*, the smallest and slowest ship in the convoy, which was following about five miles behind. Lt-Com. Biddulph signalled to her that the *Glen Usk* would be ordered to reduce speed and keep company with her, while the *Glen Gower* and *Snaefell* would proceed ahead. The leading pair passed The Lizard at 03.30 on Sunday 10th, but it was not until 11.00 that morning when the *Brighton Belle*, still accompanied by the *Glen Usk*, reached the same point. The strong easterly wind continued and the *Brighton Belle*'s commander, Lt L.K. Perrin, recorded in the log, 'Ship not making very good weather of it'. The *Glen Gower* and *Snaefell* anchored in Portland harbour at 18.45 that evening and were joined by their consorts at 08.30 on Monday 11 December. All four ships were in need of general maintenance, which was to be undertaken by Cosens & Co. of Weymouth, and during the following two days they made the short journey from Portland, through Weymouth harbour to Cosens Yard where they were to remain for about a month.

The 'straggler' of the convoy. In a rising easterly wind HMS Brighton Belle *crosses Bideford Bay on Saturday 9 December 1939. The photograph was taken from HMS* Glen Gower *after her commander had turned back to signal to her.* (Eric Rees)

HMS Glen Avon *at the Mardyke Wharf, Bristol, in December 1939, awaiting repairs by Charles Hill &* *Sons Ltd.* (Edwin Keen)

The *Glen Avon,* her repairs having been completed at Hill's Yard, left Bristol on what was to become a protracted journey to join her fellow members of the fleet at Weymouth. Her log book states:

Sunday 17 December 1939
08.00 Left Bristol.
15.05 At rendezvous off Lundy. Proceeded southward west of island.

With what ship or ships the rendezvous took place is not known but it is possible that her journey south was made in company with the *Devonia,* on the first part of her voyage from Milford Haven to the Firth of Forth.

At 23.30 that night the *Glen Avon* rounded Land's End and the early hours of the following morning found her ploughing into a SE gale and very heavy seas. She was making such slow progress across Mount's Bay that she was forced to turn back for shelter and by 09.50 she was moored in the harbour at Newlyn, where she remained for the rest of the day. By midnight the wind had moderated slightly. Her log book continues:

Tuesday 19 December 1939
00.05 Cast off from Newlyn.
01.37 Lizard abeam. Vessel plunging and pounding heavily.
10.00 Entered River Dart for shelter. Made fast to buoys.

Wednesday 20 December 1939
Stormbound at Dartmouth.

Thursday 21 December 1939
09.00 Cast off. Left River Dart. Heavy head sea.
10.20 Entered Torquay harbour for shelter.
15.00 Devonia *entered Torquay harbour for shelter and moored astern of us.*

Friday 22 December 1939
02.10 Left Torquay. Heavy swell.
11.15 Entered Portland harbour for coal.
14.30 Left Portland harbour.
16.00 Entered Weymouth harbour. Made fast alongside Town Quay.

HMS Glen Gower *at Cosens' Yard, Weymouth, early in January 1940. She is moored alongside* Snaefell, *with the* Glen Usk *astern.* (Chris Collard Collection)

HMS Brighton Belle *at Weymouth in early January 1940. The craft moored between her starboard bow and the quay is the degaussing barge, used to 'wipe' an electrical current around ships' hulls for protection against magnetic mines.* (Chris Collard Collection)

By early 1940 the maintenance of the steamers had been completed and they were ready to proceed on their journey to the Tyne. On Friday 5 January 1940 the *Glen Avon*, *Glen Gower* and *Snaefell* left Weymouth to coal at Portland and on the following day set off for Dover. They arrived at Dover, in convoy and after a rough passage, on Sunday 7th, mooring in the Wellington Dock to take on coal. They sailed at 11.30 on Monday 8th, once again in line ahead, but were delayed for a couple of hours that afternoon when they stopped to sink, with rifle fire, several drifting mines which were sighted in the vicinity of the Goodwin Sands. At 08.30 on the following morning they passed Flamborough Head and by early evening were safely berthed in the Northumberland Dock on the River Tyne.

The *Brighton Belle* and *Glen Usk* left Weymouth on Saturday 13 January 1940 and, having coaled at Portland, sailed eastward; the *Glen Usk* leaving at 18.30 and the *Brighton Belle* at 20.50. On the following afternoon the *Brighton Belle* was delayed for about five hours, near the Royal Sovereign lightvessel off Eastbourne, when she steamed into a field of drifting mines; she proceeded at 17.00 having destroyed all eight of the 'strays'. The *Glen Usk* in the meantime had forged ahead but came to a halt off Deal at 12.50 on Sunday 14th when she was forced to anchor because of thick fog. The *Brighton Belle* met with similar conditions during the night and had to anchor in The Downs.

The *Glen Usk* remained fogbound until the early afternoon of Tuesday 16th, but engine trouble then made it necessary for her to put back to Dover, where she berthed at 20.50 that evening for repairs.

The *Brighton Belle* missed the worst of the fog by steaming farther seaward but encountered some heavy weather. Nevertheless she pressed on and entered the Royal Dock, Grimsby, for coal on Tuesday 16th. Sailing again at 08.50 on Thursday 18 January, she arrived off the Tyne at 22.00 that night to await orders, and berthed in the Northumberland Dock on the following afternoon. The *Glen Usk*, her engine repairs completed, left Dover on Saturday 20th and arrived on the Tyne next day. By Tuesday 23 January 1940 all the White Funnel steamers of the 8th Flotilla were on minesweeping duties in the North Sea.

Aboard HMS Glen Gower *at Weymouth early in January 1940.* (Chris Collard Collection)

HMS Glen Gower *off Tynemouth early in 1940.* (Eric Rees)

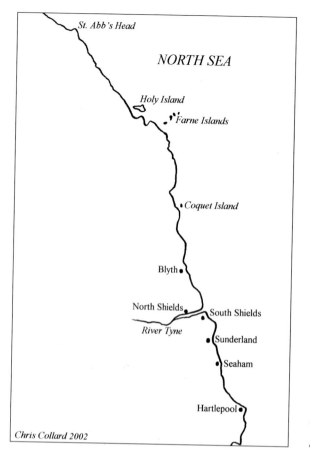

NORTH SEA

St. Abb's Head

Holy Island

Farne Islands

Coquet Island

Blyth

North Shields

South Shields

River Tyne

Sunderland

Seaham

Hartlepool

Chris Collard 2002

The principal areas of operations of the 8th Minesweeping Flotilla.

HMS Glen Usk *on the River Tyne, 1940.* (Chris Collard Collection)

From their berths in the Northumberland Dock, also the Union Quay and Fish Quay at North Shields, they swept along the coast, keeping the War Channel clear between Blyth and Sunderland. The *Glen Avon* towed the *Glen Gower* into the Tyne after she had developed engine trouble on Thursday 21 March, and on Wednesday 1 May the *Glen Avon* took divers and their equipment to the mouth of the Tyne where, in company with several naval vessels, she assisted in the location of a wreck. Otherwise, in the early months of the war, the steamers met with little incident to relieve the drudgery of their day to day routine.

Meanwhile, the ships of the 7th Flotilla reached the Firth of Forth at various intervals during January 1940, after their brief spell on the Tyne. The log of the *Westward Ho's* journey to Scottish waters states:

Monday 8 January 1940
11.30 Dep from Tyne. Sweeping northward.
17.50 Anchored off Coquet Island.

Tuesday 9 January 1940
02.00 Up anchor.
04.35 Longstone abeam.
09.00 Bass Rock abeam.
09.30 Pilot boarded off Fidra Island.
14.20 Moored in Granton after delays by fog and by examination vessel.

Thursday 11 January 1940
Began sweeping. Anchored for night off Kirkcaldy.
Sweeping to Bass Rock or St Abbs Head.

On 31 January the *Brighton Queen* was disabled after damaging her bow rudder. The *Westward Ho* stood by her until she was taken in tow to Granton by the trawler *Firefly* and the tug *Bullger*. The *Brighton Queen* was back at work after only a few days. The *Devonia*, however, was less fortunate when, having been in collision in the Forth in dense fog, she spent some time at Leith while the extensive damage was repaired. Otherwise, the daily business of clearing the channels of the Firth of Forth continued uninterrupted.

The nature of the work of the minesweepers dictated that many days were to pass without bringing tangible results, but the presence of the steamers, busily engaged on their vital task, brought comfort to seafarers by ensuring a safe passage for their ships. Winston Churchill fully appreciated their endeavours and stated:

Every day hundreds of ships went in and out of British harbours, and our survival depended upon their movement. [...] Despite many anxious periods, the mine menace was under control [...] but it was on the faithful, courageous and persistent work of the minesweepers that we chiefly relied to defeat the enemy's efforts.

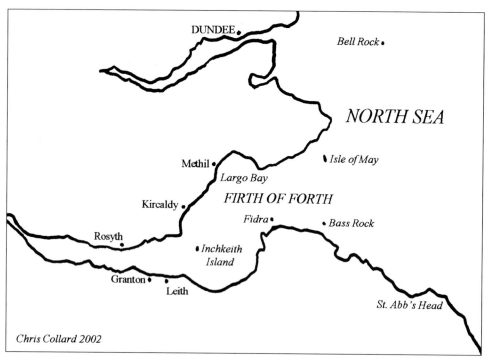

The principal areas of operations of the 7th Minesweeping Flotilla.

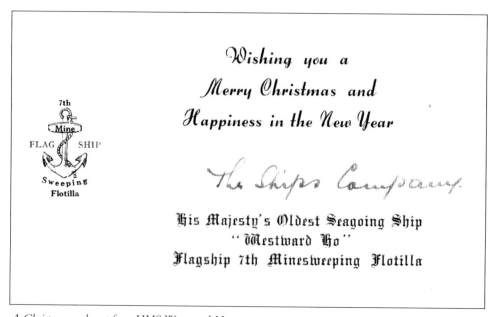

A Christmas card sent from HMS Westward Ho.

20

ROSYTH COMMAND—*continued.*

ROSYTH.		PORT EDGAR.	
M/S Base Ship.—		M/S Base Ship.—Lochinvar.	

Paddle Minesweepers.
7th Minesweeping Flotilla.

		Minesweeping Training Flotilla.	
D Westward Ho (S.O.)	At Granton.		
D Brighton Queen	At Granton.	P Syringa - - (S.O.)	Leith. Docking and Repairs. Date uncertain.
D Devonia - -	Leith. Damage Repairs. Date uncertain.	P Cypress - -'	
D Plinlimon -	Tay. At Granton.	P Cedar - -	Burntisland. Docking and Repairs. Date uncertain.
C Queen of Kent -	f.o. Sheerness.	C Laurel - -	Leith. Docking and Repairs. Date uncertain.
C Queen of Thanet	f.o. Chatham.	C Holly - -	
D Skidaw - -	At Granton.	C Magnolia -	Portsmouth (detached).
		D Sycamore -	Arrived Plymouth 13 February.

Danlaying Yachts.

Bluebird - -	Greenock. Docking and Repairs. Completes 22 February. (Allocated to Liverpool.)
Sylvana - -	

M/S Trawlers.

Hoverfly X/L -	f.o. Leith.
Lorinda X/L -	f.o. Hull.

LEITH.

Harbour Defence Patrol Craft.

E. & T.S. F -	
Fidra F -	
Floreat II F -	
Floreat III F -	
Girl Christian F -	
Girl Mary F -	

Boom Defence Vessels.

Barfair - -	
Bishopsgate -	
Craig Island -	
Cramond Island -	
Fort Ryan -	
Martinet - -	
Ocean Brine -	
Rennet - -	
River Annan -	
St. Celestin -	
Sonnet - -	
Strathspey - -	
Twinkling Star -	

Look-out Vessels.

Jubilee F - -	f.o. Leith.
Gleaners F - -	f.o. Leith.
Mistletoe F - -	
Craig F - -	
Thistle F - -	
Goodwill F - -	f.o. Leith.
Jeannie Mackay F	f.o. Leith.
Benmore F - -	f.o. Leith.

Rescue Tug.

S/S Krooman -	Boiler cleaning and repairs. Date uncertain.

A page from the Admiralty 'Red List' for early 1940. This publication appeared at intervals of about ten days throughout the war and gave details of the locations of 'Minor War Vessels in Home Waters'. (Public Records Office. Ref: ADM 208/2)

Granton Harbour early in 1940 with (left to right) Brighton Queen, Skiddaw, Devonia *and* Plinlimmon. (Chris Collard Collection)

With a coating of snow on her decks, HMS Skiddaw *steams down the Firth of Forth early in 1940.* (Chris Collard Collection)

A Ship with Mudguards

Many thousands of men risked their lives, night and day, in the minesweepers alone. [...] Their
toils and tireless courage were our salvation.

During the course of research for this book the author has been privileged to make the
acquaintance of several gentlemen who served aboard the Campbell steamers during the
Second World War.

A former Lord Mayor of Bristol, Mr Leonard Stevenson, was a bank inspector at the
outbreak of the war. His love of ships and the sea led him to volunteer for the Royal Navy.
He was drafted into the minesweeping service and joined the officers of the *Brighton Queen*.
Mr Stevenson, now at the remarkable age of ninety-six, with the assistance of his son, Alan,
recollects that the early months of the war were relatively uneventful. He recalls that the
Brighton Queen was a good sea boat; that the accommodation was comfortable and that the
food was satisfactory. When asked if there were any particular 'characters' among her
personnel he replied, 'They all were!' He also remembers the occasion of the *Devonia*'s
collision in fog in the Firth of Forth, when the *Brighton Queen* was nearby and rendered
assistance.

Mr George Arthur, of Bristol, then in his twenties, arrived in Avonmouth in the Bristol
City Line's cargo vessel *Gloucester City*, at the end of a voyage to America, shortly before the
outbreak of the war. He learned that personnel were required for the Campbell minesweepers
and signed on the *Plinlimmon* as an Engineers Assistant. In early December 1939, when she
was engaged in patrolling the Gower coast, regular gunnery practice was held. Mr Arthur
states:

> *We had experienced gunners aboard but all of the crew were ordered to try their hand. I didn't*
> *know one end of a gun from the other but I was told to have a go on the Hotchkiss gun. I did,*
> *and surprisingly found that I was quite good at it.*

His ability was put to the test early in 1940 when four German aircraft attacked several ships
of the 7th Flotilla in the Firth of Forth. Air raids were not uncommon, and although the
minesweepers were prime targets, they remained unscathed during the early months of the
war. Mr Arthur continues:

> *The* Plinlimmon *was a few miles off the coast between Fidra Island and Bass Rock, when*
> *the 'planes attacked. We opened fire and missed but succeeded in driving them off. I was about*
> *to stand down from my action station on the Hotchkiss when one of them returned, flying very*
> *low, to have another pop at us. I opened fire again and scored a direct hit! The aircraft came*
> *down on the coast at North Berwick.*

This incident was recorded in the Rosyth War Diary by the Commander in Chief:

> Friday 9 February 1940
> Plinlimmon *and* Brighton Queen *were attacked in position 330 degrees – Bass Rock 4 miles.* Plinlimmon *brought down one aircraft.* Brighton Queen *claims she shot a Heinkel down in the sea.*

The latter claim, however, was found to be incorrect. An entry for Sunday 11 February states 'It was proved today that there was no truth in *Brighton Queen's* assertion that she shot down a Heinkel in a recent raid.'

Mr Arthur's spell in the *Plinlimmon* was short. As a 'deep sea man' he found it hard to adjust to the routine of returning to port each night. He left her in March 1940 and transferred to oil tankers on the trans-Atlantic route – among the most dangerous of Merchant Navy duties. 'I survived though,' he says, 'but only just! My guardian angel must have been looking after me'.

On New Year's Day 1940, Leslie Rashleigh, a sixteen-year-old Royal Naval Volunteer Reserve Signalman, having completed his initial training at Skegness, joined his first ship – HMS *Devonia*. It had taken him three days to find her. From his home in Cornwall he made his way to Devonport where he was told that she had put into Portland for coal. On arrival at Portland he found that he had missed her, but was advised that as she was to be placed under Rosyth command, he would find her there. He made the long journey north to the Scottish dockyard only to find that she had not yet arrived but was probably coaling in the Tyne area. Eventually he tracked her down; she had put into West Hartlepool. Mr Rashleigh reported on board a mere two hours before she sailed for Granton at about midday. In the darkness of that evening her commander, unsure of his exact position, sighted a trawler and approached her to within hailing distance. The trawler skipper told him that he was north of May Island at the entrance to the Firth of Forth; he was heading that way and if the commander would care to follow, he would lead him into Granton.

Mr Rashleigh recalls life on board in the early days of the war:

> *With the Oropesa minesweeping gear fitted aft, the* Devonia *had a single 12-pounder gun on the foredeck and Lewis gun mountings on each paddle box; the usual armament for the excursion paddlers. All the large saloon windows were plated over, the after saloon on the main deck becoming the wardroom and officers quarters. All other personnel were accommodated in two messes in what was the forward saloon on the main deck, with seamen on the starboard side, and the Maltese engine room and stokehold hands to port. On the lower deck were the petty officers and leading hands. As ships designed for summer operations, few had any sort of heating but this was remedied by the installation of cast-iron stoves, whose chimneys went straight up through the deckhead. Apart from the skipper, only the steamer's telegraphist lived in comparative luxury, in the wireless cabin below the bridge.*
>
> *The* Devonia's *crew consisted of the commander; first lieutenant; a sub-lieutenant RNVR; chief engineer (lieutenant RNR); second engineer (sub-lieutenant RNR); coxswain (petty officer, pensioner); chief petty officer; leading hands (one RN and one RNR); three able seamen (all RN); petty officer steward; petty officer cook; telegraphist (RNVR); signalman*

(RNVR); twelve Maltese from Cardiff for engine room and stokehold duties; five Hull and three Stornoway fishermen.

We swept daily, usually in company with the Devonia's sister ship, the Brighton Queen. After leaving Granton and passing through the boom defence from Inchkeith Island to the north shore of the Forth, we proceeded to just off Methil, a rendezvous point for the east coast convoys. There we streamed our sweeps and followed the shipping channel. Sometimes the Brighton Queen broke off and went north of May Island to off Dundee, but we always took the southern channel past Bass Rock towards St Abbs Head before hauling in sweeps and making for home. Occasionally we ventured farther south and anchored for the night inside the Farne Islands.

In view of the difficult entrance to Granton harbour our skipper was always anxious to get back while it was still light. This called for full speed, which in the Devonia's case was quite considerable. She must have made an awesome sight with her two funnels giving forth vast clouds of black smoke!

Life on board was quite monotonous. We were in harbour most nights, which was fortunate, as on those occasions when we anchored 'outside' we usually found the odd mine floating around the hull, having broken adrift from our own field. In my time with the Devonia, however, we never swept a single mine, her cutters somehow seeming inadequate.

Luckily, Mr Rashleigh had the foresight to take his camera with him, and the photographs of his shipmates, reproduced in this volume, are an invaluable record of life on board. However, he greatly regrets a photographic opportunity which he missed. He was on shore leave while the *Devonia* was out of action undergoing routine boiler and tube cleaning. While walking through Granton he had stopped to enjoy the view down the Firth of Forth when four of the *Devonia's* consorts came steaming in from seaward at full speed. Mr Rashleigh states:

They were in line ahead but suddenly turned together and approached the harbour head on. With their wide sponsons and smoke belching from their funnels as they churned their way across the Forth, they looked like battleships in miniature. They made such an impressive sight that it was hard to believe that these were the same ships which carried passengers on their summer outings to the seaside. I could have kicked myself for leaving my camera behind. The finest photograph I never took!

During the spring of 1940, in between minesweeping operations, the *Devonia* was occasionally used to ferry soldiers from Granton to the troopships in the Firth of Forth waiting to take them across the North Sea to engage the German forces following their attack on Norway. Towards the end of the ill-fated campaign the *Devonia* took a full complement of troops to board the requisitioned P&O passenger liner, *Oriana*. On the following day the Scandinavian operation had virtually ended and the *Devonia* was ordered to disembark her contingent and return them to Granton. While alongside the *Oriana* a soldier stepped off the accommodation ladder onto the *Devonia's* deck, looked at her two paddle boxes and exclaimed, 'Oh. A ship with mudguards!'

Aboard HMS *Devonia* in the spring of 1940

On the journey down the east coast to Harwich, on Wednesday 29 May, ready to take part in the Dunkirk evacuation. From top, in the lifeboat: 'Lofty' Elletson; 'Ginger' Graham; A. Needham; E. Fell; 'Sparks'; Jim Houghton; A. McLeod. Leaning against the lifeboat is the Coxswain. (Leslie Rashleigh)

Standing, left to right: Jock McTaggart; 'Ginger' Graham; ? McDonald; E. Fell; 'Gaz' Gasson; the Coxswain; T. Hammett; Jim Houghton; Tim Lacey. Sitting: A. McLeod; 'Sparks'; 'Lofty' Elletson; A. Needham. (Leslie Rashleigh)

Above:: *Jim Houghton, one of the* Devonia's *six Hull fishermen, at the sweeping winch on the after deck.* (Leslie Rashleigh)

Right: *'Sweeps out' – Streaming Oropesa floats.* (Leslie Rashleigh)

The bridge, wheelhouse and upper bridge.
(Leslie Rashleigh)

'Gaz' Gasson, complete with his personalised bucket, scrubbing his hammock. 'Gaz' was unlucky; he was due to be discharged from his Royal Naval National Service on the day on which war broke out. (Leslie Rashleigh)

Right: *The Devonia's Second in Command, Lt Charles Cox RNVR, checks the Lewis gun on the starboard paddle box.* (Leslie Rashleigh)

Below: *One 'watch' of HMS Devonia's twelve Maltese stokers. Back row, left to right: E. Galea; A. Feneck; Joe Brincat. Front row: G. Fittini; C. Galea; Tony Cacciotolo, holding 'Queenie', the Commander's dog; Carmello Vassallo.* (Leslie Rashleigh)

With HMS *Glen Gower* on the North East Coast

On the evening of Monday 13 May 1940, a memorable event was witnessed by the personnel of HMS Glen Gower, *while lying at the Fish Quay, North Shields. The destroyer HMS* Kelly, *under the command of Capt. Louis Mountbatten, had been torpedoed of Sylt Island, near the Danish coast, on the night of Friday 10 May 1940. In a sinking condition, her flotilla consort, HMS* Bulldog *(right) towed her across the North Sea until tugs took over at the entrance to the Tyne.* (Eric Rees)

Capt. Louis Mountbatten, having spent ninety-two hours without rest, is visible on HMS Kelly's *starboard bridge wing, as she is manoeuvred upriver to Hawthorne Leslie's Yard at Hebburn. The Rosyth War Diary states: 'HMS* Kelly *was finally brought into the Tyne for repairs after a three day struggle against – not only natural elements – but also enemy aircraft.'* (Eric Rees)

Above and below: *Aboard HMS* Glen Gower, *bringing in a sweep in heavy weather near Holy Island, off the Northumberland coast, in 1940.* (Eric Rees)

Trouble Brewing

While the monotonous but vital work of the Campbell steamers continued, the 48th General Meeting of P&A Campbell Ltd was held at the Grand Hotel, Bristol, on 16 May 1940. In his report to the shareholders the chairman, Mr G.H. Boucher, stated:

> Our organisation is being kept alive but, of course, it is simply a skeleton of its normal character. [...]
>
> With regard to the future, we have transformed ourselves from a peace-time to a war-time footing. [...]
>
> Last summer seems a very long time ago but if you will cast your minds back you will remember that, so far as the weather was concerned, we have seldom met with such a protracted period of bad weather as we then experienced. Right up to August we had no summer at all, but that month was, from every point of view, satisfactory. September was a wonderful month but unfortunately we had to withdraw all our ships in the first few days of that month owing to the outbreak of the war, and we lost all the receipts which we otherwise should have obtained in a month of almost perfect summer weather. [...]
>
> As you are all aware, shortly after the outbreak of the war over ninety-percent of our fleet was requisitioned by the government. I am not at liberty to say for what purpose the vessels were requisitioned, how they are being utilised or where they are, but they are satisfactorily carrying out such duties as they are called upon to exercise by the Admiralty.

The chairman ended his report by saying, 'As far as I am aware, up to last night, all the vessels were in being, undamaged and unhurt.' That statement was soon to acquire a greater significance and poignancy than anyone could have imagined. The steamers of the White Funnel Fleet were about to take part in the greatest evacuation in military history!

Dunkirk – The Lost Steamers

The House should prepare itself for hard and heavy tidings. [...] Nothing that may happen in this battle can in any way relieve us of our duty to defend the world cause to which we have vowed ourselves.

Operation Dynamo

Thousands of soldiers of the British Expeditionary Force and their French comrades had been forced to retreat eastwards towards the coast after the German army swept into northern France on the morning of 10 May 1940. After the fall of Boulogne and Calais, only one port, and its neighbouring beaches, remained in Allied hands; a port whose origins lay in a small village built around a church in the sand – the church of the dunes – Dunkirk.

By Tuesday 28 May the Allies had established a perimeter of defence around Dunkirk stretching from Nieuport, along the canals through Furnes and Bergues, to Gravelines. Into this pocket the exhausted Allies retreated steadily along congested roads until, by midnight on Wednesday 29 May, the greater part of the BEF and nearly half of the French 1st Army lay within the canal line. By this time the Naval measures for their evacuation were well under way.

An appeal for small and shallow-draught vessels of all types had been issued on Friday 24 May, and over the following days a vast number of such craft converged on the ports of south-east England to await orders.

In overall charge of the operation was Vice-Admiral Bertram Ramsay, a quietly spoken, unassuming man, small in stature but a giant in terms of planning. His office, cut into the chalk cliffs at Dover, had housed an auxiliary lighting system for the castle; it was known as 'The Dynamo Room' and gave its name to the operation. From what has been described as a 'motley armada', Vice-Admiral Ramsay assembled as disparate and formidable a rescue fleet as could be imagined. His organisation and leadership led to the execution of one of the most remarkable achievements in British maritime history – Operation Dynamo.

Capt. William Tennant was appointed Senior Naval Officer in charge of the shore end of the evacuation and supervised the distribution and loading of the rescue fleet. Offshore, the former Battleship Commander, Rear-Admiral Frederic Wake-Walker, controlled the flow of shipping.

The first day of the evacuation – Monday 27 May 1940 – proved to be disappointing; only 7,669 troops were brought out. For the rescuers, entering Dunkirk harbour was a dangerous task. In addition to contending with air attacks and long range fire from the German shore batteries, they had to negotiate many wrecks that lay between the open sea and the burning town. It became apparent that the hungry, exhausted troops would have to be embarked from the sandy beaches on either side of the town. Vice-Admiral Ramsay had few small craft capable of embarking men in the shallow water of the gently sloping beaches but he signalled for more and his call was speedily answered.

On the following day, Tuesday 28 May, using the beaches as well as the 1,400yd-long east mole of the harbour, 17,804 men were embarked for Great Britain. The losses in craft that day were, however, very heavy. The ships which left the mole unscathed were frequently damaged or sunk by bombing as they steamed down the narrow offshore channel, unable to manoeuvre adequately for wrecks and debris.

A total of 47,310 men were snatched from Dunkirk on Wednesday 29 May, but during the course of the day, as soon as the wind blew aside the pall of smoke obscuring the harbour and roadstead, the Luftwaffe wrought havoc with a concentrated bombardment of the mole, sinking three destroyers and twenty-one other vessels.

On Thursday 30 May, however, smoother seas, smoke and low cloud enabled the rescuers to remove 13,823 men.

On Friday 31 May, despite intense bombing and shelling, a staggering 68,014 troops were removed to safety, but on the following day a furious artillery bombardment and strafing of the whole length of the beaches, together with a resolute dive-bombing of shipping out at sea and in the harbour, effectively put an end to daylight operations.

The climax of the evacuation had taken place on 31 May and 1 June, when over 132,000 troops were landed in England. At dawn on 2 June only 4,000 men of the British Expeditionary Force remained in the perimeter, shielded by 100,000 French troops. On the nights of 2 and 3 June the British were evacuated along with 60,000 Frenchmen. Dunkirk was still defended stubbornly by the remainder who resisted until the morning of 4 June. When the town fell 40,000 French troops, who had fought tenaciously to cover the evacuation of their Allied comrades, marched into captivity.

Eight of the ten requisitioned White Funnel steamers took part in the evacuation; the exceptions were the *Glen Usk* and the *Skiddaw*. The former was undergoing a refit at Brigham & Cowan's Yard in the Albert Edward Dock, on the River Tyne, which withdrew her from service from Saturday 25 May to Monday 3 June, by which time the evacuation was virtually over. The *Skiddaw* had been undergoing boiler cleaning at Rosyth but as soon as this had been completed she took on coal and sailed from Granton on Friday 31 May, arriving at Harwich two days later. The Flag Officer in Charge considered it advisable to hold her in reserve; in the event, however, she was not required, and took no part in the evacuation.

HMS *Brighton Belle*

The first of the White Funnel steamers to arrive on the French coast was the diminutive *Brighton Belle*. She had been transferred from the 8th to the 10th Flotilla in late March 1940 and sailed from her base at Dover on the evening of Monday 27 May. Having embarked about 350 troops, she left Dunkirk early on the following morning and all went well until she approached the English coast. Lt L.K. Perrin's report to Admiral Ramsay gives the details of subsequent events:

> *I regret to inform you that HMS* Brighton Belle *sank at 13.00 on 28 May 1940 in a position south of the Gull Buoy, off Ramsgate, as a result of striking a submerged object in The Downs, 3 cables, 183 degrees from the Gull Buoy at 12.30. The ship was taken in tow*

by an examination tug after the troops had been transferred to other vessels, but the effort to save her was futile. Brighton Belle was returning from the French coast and had on board approximately 350 men of the British Army who had been evacuated earlier in the day. At the time of the accident I was closing Ramsgate for orders regarding disembarkation of the troops, and as an air attack was in progress I was concerned about the number of army people about the upper deck. This caused a relaxation on my part in the conning of the ship, the loss of which, I can only state, was due to an error of judgement. There were no casualties.

It was later discovered that the *Brighton Belle* had struck the submerged wreck of a ship which had been sunk earlier by a magnetic mine. A large part of her bottom had been torn away and she sank by the stern until she rested on a sandbank. All of her officers and crew, including the commander's dog, were rescued by her 10th Flotilla consort, the New Medway Steam Packet Co.'s paddle steamer *Medway Queen*.

HMS *Brighton Queen*

The *Brighton Queen*, *Plinlimmon* and *Westward Ho* sailed from Granton on Tuesday 28 May and arrived at Harwich on Thursday 30. The *Brighton Queen*, in company with a number of paddle steamers from the Dover-based 10th Flotilla, left for France later that day and headed for La Panne, the small Belgian resort ten miles east of Dunkirk. Her telegraphist, Mr Arthur Blakeburn, in a subsequent press interview, takes up the story:

At dusk we were attacked by some enemy aircraft flying fairly high, which dropped bombs well wide of us. We opened fire with our twelve-pounder, but we missed them as much as they missed us.

On arrival off La Panne before dawn on Friday 31 May we anchored near the shore, lowered our boats and the crew went off to review the situation. They returned with a boatload of soldiers and transferred them to the Brighton Queen.

Daylight arrived and then the fireworks started; we were not under continuous attack but it seemed like it, and then the boats began to shuttle between the beach and the ship. Any boat to any ship seemed to be the plan but I shall never forget the orderly queues of troops up to their chests in water, waiting for a lift, ducking as the bombs exploded in the water or on the beach.

Apart from helping the men aboard from the small boats I spent a lot of time re-arming the Lewis gun which was mounted on deck outside the radio cabin. I don't recall being fed at all!

When we had embarked about 600 troops we set off for Dover. I had six soldiers sleeping on the deck of the radio cabin and two on my bunk; they had been dug in at La Panne for three days. We were attacked and 'near missed' on the way back but no great damage was done. The sea was wonderfully smooth and we made good time to Dover. [...]

While returning to England the *Brighton Queen* took in tow a Dutch coaster which was disabled with defective engines. The coaster, with 500 troops crammed aboard, was towed stern first for several miles by which time the engineers had restarted her engines and the tow

53

was slipped. During this time both vessels were attacked by enemy aircraft but escaped with only minor damage.

Mr Blakeburn continues:

We were soon on our way back to Dunkirk. This time we set off in beautiful weather on the morning of 1 June at a good rate of knots. We survived three air attacks on the way and it wasn't long before we reached Dunkirk, with its oil tanks burning furiously. Dunkirk harbour was protected by two moles, east and west, this time we berthed at the east mole and immediately the troops began to board. All the time the harbour was under attack from the air and from inland; it was about this time that we were attacked by dive bombers – something I remember with a shudder.

I was helping troops to board when I heard a screaming noise. I couldn't pin it down at first but I soon realised what it was when the bombs started exploding. I had heard about these screaming Stukas from other crews but this was my first experience of them and it scared me stiff! The planes were aiming for both moles and were having some success, but we carried on loading the troops which included Frenchmen and Moroccans. As they came aboard we were trying to indicate that they should remove their greatcoats and packs; some of them did and it turned out that they were the lucky ones.

When we had a full load – about 700 this time – we set off. I was making my way to the bridge to see if there were any messages to send and we must have been four or five miles from the mole, when a major air attack began. I saw three aircraft plummeting down and the next thing was an almighty crash astern. I ducked and when I looked up I saw bits of wreckage and bodies coming down. The bomb, or bombs, must have gone through the deck and exploded below the waterline because the ship began to sink immediately. I went into the radio cabin to switch on the transmitter but the water rapidly became waist deep and I got out quickly. By the time I had inflated my lifejacket and kicked off my boots I was afloat and swimming away from the ship. Suddenly I had thoughts about the boiler exploding and made my own rapid rate of knots from the doomed Brighton Queen.

Many of the soldiers were gunned down in the sea with machine gun fire and many were drowned. Some, I think, would have lived if they had removed their greatcoats and packs. After swimming for a while I lay on my back and looked up at the beautiful sky; I hoped that if and when I was picked up it would be by a ship going home rather than one going to Dunkirk. After a while the frigate, Saltash, *came alongside with her scramble nets down and lifelines over the side. I was up and over pretty smartish and once again found myself helping survivors aboard. A few hours later we berthed at Margate pier. I had taken off my clothes and put them in the boiler room of the* Saltash *for a quick dry-out, but they had disappeared when I went to collect them, so a friendly matelot gave me a towel. My return to England found me walking down Margate pier, dressed only in the towel but with my moneybelt still around my waist. I didn't care – I was just very thankful to be out of it!*

The *Brighton Queen* had sailed from Dunkirk just before noon. Twenty minutes later, off the Dyck Shoal, the bombing attack began and she was struck by one 500lb bomb aft of the starboard paddle box. She sank within seven minutes with the loss of half of her complement. Her second-in-command, the P&A Campbell master, Capt. William Watson, was one of the last men to leave her, and spent over two hours in the water clinging to the top of her mast before he was rescued.

HMS *Devonia*

Signalman Leslie Rashleigh recalls the *Devonia*'s part in the evacuation:

On the night of Tuesday 28 May 1940 we were anchored inside the Farne Islands, off the Northumberland coast. I was roused from my hammock by the look-out, who had seen a light flashing from the shore. I answered and received a curt 'Please man your RT' instruction in return. Having awoken the telegraphist we received a signal at 23.00 for the captain's eyes only, and at midnight we set off to coal at Tynemouth. We then continued southwards along the coast in marvellous weather and eventually berthed at Harwich at 14.00 on Thursday 30 May. The harbour was so unusually congested with vessels of all types that we wondered what was going on. A fresh arrival from Dunkirk came alongside us and painted a lurid picture of what was in store; although we had never heard of the place, it was obviously going to be no picnic!

We coaled ready for an early start on the morning of Friday 31 May and sailed along the Essex and Kent coasts until reaching the swept channel across to France. By this time there was considerable two-way traffic and in addition to tugs towing long strings of motor cruisers and launches I remember seeing a French destroyer crossing to England, stern first, with heavy damage forward.

We passed Dunkirk and continued along the coast to La Panne where a commodore came aboard to brief the captain. He left in his boat and we moved slowly in towards the beaches, which seemed to be alive with soldiers trying to get off in small boats. This was made difficult by the surf which, although not very heavy, tended to beach the boats and strand them. At one stage lorries had been driven into the sea in an attempt to form a makeshift jetty – not very successfully apparently.

There was a lot of air activity, mainly bombing, and the Germans were also near Nieuport, which they shelled spasmodically. We manned the twelve-pounder and the Lewis gun, which helped morale if nothing else. We launched our boats to make a couple of runs inshore, off-loading the troops on to the Hilda, *a small, one hold, high pooped Dutch coaster manned by a Royal Naval lieutenant and three ratings. Before long the bombing and shelling came too close for comfort and we reeled from a stick of bombs which fell immediately behind us. They opened up the Devonia's stern plates and before long the commodore re-appeared to speak to our captain, Lt J. Brotchie.*

Owing to the severity of the damage we were instructed to beach the ship as far in as possible in the hope that she would act as a breakwater to help in the embarkation of wounded troops. The enemy, however, frustrated this plan with repeated aircraft attacks, and the Devonia had to be abandoned. When the order to abandon ship was given the Chief Petty Officer passed amongst us with the rum jar and everyone was told to take a stiff tot in case we ended up in the sea. I then took the ship's confidential books and papers to the stokehold to be burned. The second engineer and I were the last to leave the poor Devonia; he was not a happy man as he opened up the seacocks. We then left in style after our unfinished day trip to France by rowing across to the Hilda, *before being transferred to the destroyer* Scimitar *and returning to Dover.*

By way of comparison, part of Lt Brotchie's official report to the Admiralty is quoted:

Friday 31 May 1940.
03.00 Departed from Harwich and proceeded to La Panne, where we anchored at about mid-day. The ship was shelled and bombed continuously, one salvo of four bombs falling within a few feet of our stern, causing extensive damage to the hull.
16.00 Commodore in Charge boarded and gave verbal instruction to beach ship.

A slight discrepancy then occurs in Lt Brotchie's report. He states:

06.00 Vessel was beached at full speed in position given. All ammunition, charts etc. of a confidential nature were burned in my presence. The officers and crew are to be complimented on their magnificent fight throughout; discipline was perfect.

The time of '06.00' is inconsistent with the rest of the report, which was scribbled, at the time, in pencil on several scraps of paper. In the mayhem and confusion prevailing around him it appears likely that the ship was beached at 6.00 p.m. and he simply entered the time in the wrong form. His next entry would seem to support this view:

At 19.30 on 31/5, the shelling and bombing being dangerous, the order to abandon ship was given. This was done quietly and well, the crew going to several ships detailed for evacuation purposes. Twelve officers and men, and one dog disembarked (including myself) only when nothing else was to be done. Guns spiked, W/T apparatus etc. destroyed, sea-cocks opened.

Several facts concerning the beaching of the *Devonia* were brought to light by Petty Officer Wilcox, of HMS *Westward Ho*, in the years after the war. He stated that, quite early during the evacuation, the decision had been made to beach one of the paddle steamers to act as an embarkation stage. This particular type of vessel was decided upon as they were the only ships of any size which were flat-bottomed. In fact, at 10.35 on 31 May, Admiral Wake-Walker had signalled to the Vice Admiral at Dover that he intended to beach a ship, 'in the hope of improving conditions for embarking troops'. The Vice Admiral replied that this course of action was approved. As the chosen vessel would be unlikely to survive the ordeal, consideration was given as to which one was the most expendable. The *Westward Ho* was detailed for this sad duty, possibly because she was the oldest paddle steamer taking part in the evacuation. She had arrived off La Panne at about the same time as the *Devonia*, and the *Westward Ho's* commander had actually been given the order to beach her. However, at the time she was embarking troops from the beach and owing to difficulties in handling the boats in the surf a considerable delay occurred in carrying out the order. It appears that, in the meantime, the matter was then reconsidered as the *Devonia* had been experiencing a great deal of engine trouble during the previous few weeks. Before the final decision was made, fate intervened when the Luftwaffe's bombs opened up the *Devonia's* stern plates and rendered her unseaworthy; she was the obvious choice.

The order for her to be beached was given by Rear Admiral Wake-Walker, then flying his flag in the destroyer HMS *Keith*, at anchor offshore. It was passed to Lt Brotchie by Commodore Gilbert Stephenson, a sixty-two-year-old retired Vice Admiral under Capt. Tennant's command, who was assisting operations in the yacht *Bounty*, off La Panne. A paragraph of the Commodore's report to the Rear Admiral states:

> *In accordance with your instructions and after consultation with Army Embarkation Officers, I ordered HMS* Devonia *to beach herself at La Panne.*

The problems of the *Devonia* came to the attention of Mr Keen at Bristol, who later wrote:

> *I was told that the* Devonia *was more or less a failure in this war. Her year out of service did her no good at all. There was always something or other wrong with her and she did very little actual steaming. For this reason she was chosen to be 'thrown away'. I am very vexed about this, and also the loss of the* Brighton Queen; *two large, sea-going paddle steamers the like of which we shall never see again.*

Thus, the *Devonia* was abandoned, along with many other vessels which ended their days on the Dunkirk beaches.

Her story, however, does not end there. On Thursday 14 April 1949 the Bristol *Evening World* published an article headed 'The Mystery of the *Devonia* – Is a former Bristol pleasure steamer in service on a German river?'

The 'mystery' was under investigation by a resident of Weston-super-Mare, who put forward two assertions – that the *Devonia* was still intact at the end of the war, and that she had been salvaged and put to use somewhere in Germany.

His first assertion was based on the photograph reproduced on page 60. He stated that the soldier nearest the camera is wearing an American uniform and that the photograph was, therefore, probably taken after D-Day, when the Allied troops were pushing through Belgium towards Holland. The photograph, however, is heavily retouched and is, consequently, somewhat unreliable as evidence.

The newspaper article continues:

> *Reports have reached me that the* Devonia *was still on the beach four years after the evacuation of Dunkirk, when we invaded the Continent. I have spoken to troops who say they actually saw her there.*

His enquiries suffered a setback when, in response to a letter, the Mayor of Dunkirk informed him that as far as he knew, after the evacuation the Germans stripped the *Devonia* and the many other wrecks and took away the material for their own war effort.

This view, however, was not borne out by Messrs Allen and Keen; the latter writing on 28 July 1944:

> *An airman informs me that the* Devonia *is still to be seen on the shore near Dunkirk and, from a distance, appears quite orderly. I suspect, however, that her hull is badly suffering from the effects of gales and neglect.*

One wonders how reliable the airman was at ship recognition, but it should be added that Mr Allen was not given to making statements without substantiation. It is quite certain that he would have had good grounds for endorsing such information.

Mr Keen, in a letter to the author in 1965, stated:

> *Of course we shall never know exactly what happened to her but I am pretty certain that she was not broken up where she lay, but was refloated and taken away somewhere. I remember H.A. Allen writing that an airman told him that she suddenly disappeared from the beach.*

The Weston-super-Mare resident concluded his newspaper article by stating that he was convinced that the *Devonia* was in service somewhere on the Continent, possibly on the Rhine, Elbe or Seine, and that he would continue his investigations until he could prove it!

To add fuel to the fire, a correspondent wrote to the *Evening World* on 31 May 1949:

> *Plying between Leer and Borkum, one of the little islands at the mouth of the Ems, is a ship which I am convinced is the* Devonia. *She is being operated under the name* Prince Wilhelm.

The correspondent was at home in Bristol, on leave from his employment on port control work at Emden, and stated that he knew the *Devonia* well. He had been on board the *Prince Wilhelm* and was convinced that they were one and the same ship. He added that on his return to Emden he would look further into the matter.

To what extent these gentlemen pursued their enquiries is not known, but nothing more was heard from either, and no evidence has ever been produced to support the theory that she sailed again.

In conclusion it would be appropriate to quote the late Grahame Farr, the eminent shipping historian, who states in his book, *West Country Passenger Steamers*:

> *Rumours were current that she was salved and later ran a passenger service on one of the German rivers, but searches by many enthusiasts have failed to substantiate this suggestion.*

The mystery of the fate of the *Devonia* is one which will probably never be conclusively solved.

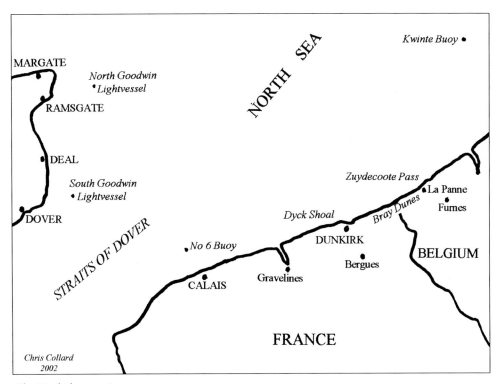

The Dunkirk evacuation area.

HMS Brighton Belle *sinking off Ramsgate on Tuesday 28 May 1940. Her stern rests on a sandbank while the last of her crew prepare to abandon her.* (Chris Collard Collection)

Above and below: *HMS* Devonia *ashore at* La Panne. (Chris Collard Collection)

HMS Devonia *ashore at La Panne. In the background can be seen the abandoned Thames paddle steamer,* Crested Eagle. (Chris Collard Collection)

DUNKIRK – THE SURVIVORS

When it was known how many men had been rescued from Dunkirk a sense of deliverance spread in the island and throughout the Empire.

Southward from the Tyne

During the course of their minesweeping duties on the late afternoon of Tuesday 28 May 1940, the *Glen Avon*, *Glen Gower* and *Snaefell* were ordered to return to harbour immediately to take on coal. At 23.30 that night they cleared the breakwaters of the River Tyne and steamed southward in convoy, mooring in Harwich on the morning of Thursday 30 May; the *Snaefell* at Trinity Pier and the others at Parkeston Quay.

The following account of their subsequent actions includes details from the official report submitted, on 3 June 1940, to the Flag Officer in Charge at Harwich by Acting Commander Biddulph, the senior officer of the 8th Minesweeping Flotilla:

> *Sir,*
>
> *I have the honour to submit this, my letter of proceedings in connection with the evacuation of troops of the BEF from Dunkirk.*
>
> *During the forenoon of 30 May 1940 I was in receipt of a signal from V.A. at Dover to proceed to beaches 8 miles east of Dunkirk and evacuate troops, and to sail at noon. The two other ships of the flotilla under my command, HMS* Glen Avon *and HMS* Snaefell, *at present at Harwich, were in receipt of a similar signal.*
>
> *As the ships had only arrived at Harwich at 07.45 the same morning it was not possible to complete coaling, watering and provisioning by this time, and the necessary charts had to be drawn and the route obtained. All this was pushed forward with the utmost despatch however. Extra tinned beef, bread and butter were drawn for feeding the troops and the three vessels left at 13.45.*
>
> *I had spoken with the Commanding Officer of HMS* Oriole *[the Clyde paddle steamer* Eagle III*], which had arrived that forenoon from a similar expedition, and he was able to give me some valuable information as a result of his experiences. On leaving Harwich I addressed the ship's company and told them what we were going to do and how I proposed to do it, at the same time informing them that anyone's ideas would be considered and used if good. I also warned them that in view of the limited fresh water capacity of the ship and the fact that we must have plenty for the troops, water must be used sparingly and that washing would be a punishable offence. This raised a cheer.*
>
> *The flotilla proceeded in company but I made a signal to each ship to proceed independently at her utmost speed and to act in accordance with orders received, telling them briefly what I proposed to do myself.* Glen Gower *was soon left behind as she is somewhat the slowest ship*

and I felt rather like the Duke of Plaza Toro who led his regiment from behind, though not with the same intentions. [See the Gilbert and Sullivan opera The Gondoliers.*] I did not lose sight of them however.*

By 18.45 we had altered course into the main channel for Dunkirk and found ourselves in company with vessels of all types on the same errand, while others were coming back laden with troops. The alarm was sounded several times in sighting or hearing aircraft but these all proved to be British.

At 20.58 we turned to run along the coast past Dunkirk. Gunfire could be heard and a large fire was blazing in Dunkirk itself sending up thick columns of smoke which hung about like a pall over the beleaguered city. We passed Dunkirk light at 21.17. At 21.21 heavy artillery fire was heard ahead and the tracers from Bofors guns could be seen streaking into the sky. Bombs could be seen exploding on the beaches and in the water close to. The noise of aeroplane engines could be heard but we could not see the planes themselves.

The *Snaefell*, some distance ahead of the *Glen Gower*, was in action against the enemy aircraft between 21.20 and 21.40. Bombs were dropped ahead and astern of her, but despite the fact that her commander, Lt Frank Brett, was unable to manoeuvre the ship owing to the many wrecks in the narrow channel, she was undamaged and anchored off La Panne at 22.00.

Cdr Biddulph's report continues:

We passed a number of sunken vessels of various types and a burned out paddle steamer [The General Steam Navigation Co.'s *Crested Eagle*] *on the shore.*

At 21.24 an enemy aircraft was seen and three rounds were fired from the 12 pounder. As, however, no attack developed upon the ship I gave the order to cease fire, deeming it advisable to save our limited amount of ammunition for short barrage defence against dive bombing aircraft actually attacking the ship.

At 21.37 troops could be heard shouting ashore but we had not yet reached our destination. At 21.40 more heavy artillery fire was put up from destroyers and shore batteries.

At 22.10 I came to anchor in 5 fathoms off the beach approximately 8 miles east of Dunkirk. The tide was now ebbing. Glen Avon and Snaefell were anchored either side of me. The two boats were lowered and sent straight inshore, one with a party of ratings and one officer, Lieut. Johnson RNVR, and the other with Lieut. Chapman RNVR in charge. By this time it was completely dark. At 23.30 the first boat came back laden with British troops, followed closely by the second. The coxswains reported great difficulty in refloating the boats owing to the rapidly falling tide and the very gradual slope of the beach. The soldiers were tired and disinclined to help to get the boats off. In view of the fact that I intended to beach the ship soon after the turning of the tide at 02.20 I decided to stop sending in the ship's boats for fear of getting them stranded. In the meantime, however, there was a more or less steady stream of troops arriving by the local flat-bottomed boats. Tea and sandwiches were served to them as they arrived after which they mostly fell into the sleep of exhaustion.

I weighed anchor at 02.05 and ran the ship into the beach, taking the ground at 02.20. The kedge anchor was laid out to prevent the stern swinging in. The idea of beaching was that ladders and hawsers, hanging alongside, would be used by the troops to climb aboard, after wading out to the bows. This idea proved to be impracticable, the ship being still some way from

Above and below: *At 05.30 on Friday 31 May 1940 HMS* Snaefell, *with 583 troops aboard, leaves the Dunkirk beaches bound for Harwich.* (Chris Collard Collection)

the water's edge. The embarkation was therefore continued by means of the ship's boats in the charge of seamen coxswains; the two lieutenants being retained aboard to assist in the distribution and tallying of the troops. In the meantime the ship became hard and fast broadside to the beach owing to the fact that the kedge anchor had dragged. The stokers assisted in the boats to relieve the seamen crews and the work of embarkation proceeded steadily by the ship's boats and flat-bottomed craft propelled by the soldiers themselves.

By 04.25 we had embarked 530 troops. I then received orders from Vice Admiral, Dover, passed by a destroyer farther out, and addressed to all paddle minesweepers to proceed alongside Dunkirk pier. Snaefell, *in response to my signal, towed my stern clear, and with assistance from the engines the ship was soon afloat.*

The *Snaefell* had taken 583 soldiers aboard. The mess decks of her petty officers, seamen and stokers were readily turned over to the troops. Lt Brett's accommodation provided a resting place for fifteen army officers and a further thirty were allocated to the officers' dining room. Being filled to capacity, at 05.00 she left her anchorage, assisted the *Glen Gower* to reach deep water and at 05.20 proceeded direct to Harwich, where she arrived alongside Parkeston Quay at 13.05.

The *Glen Avon*, like the *Glen Gower*, had also been beached, and at 05.25, having taken aboard her full complement, had been aground for just over an hour. The tide was now on the flood but it was not without difficulty that she was refloated. While heaving down the beach on her kedge anchor she was attacked by enemy aircraft but escaped damage. Her starboard anchor cable then parted and her port anchor became fouled, but her commander, Lt B. Loyns, was not inclined to delay his departure to retrieve them. As soon as she refloated, at about 05.50, she proceeded to Harwich in the wake of the *Snaefell*, arriving alongside Parkeston Quay at 15.20.

HMS Glen Avon *leaving Dunkirk on Friday 31 May 1940.* (Chris Collard Collection)

In the wake of the Snaefell, *the* Glen Avon *sets off across the English Channel.* (Chris Collard Collection)

HMS Glen Avon *arriving at Harwich on the afternoon of Friday 31 May 1940.* (Chris Collard Collection)

Right and below: *Aboard HMS Snaefell arriving at Harwich on the afternoon of Friday 31 May 1940.* (Ken Jenkins Collection)

Cdr Biddulph's report continues:

At 05.20, having hoisted the boats, I proceeded for Dunkirk. The shore party, who had come off and gone in again in a flat-bottomed boat for another load, were left behind, but I knew that they would make for the Glen Avon *on our departure, as she did not proceed until about half an hour later, by which time she was full and carried on direct to Harwich.*

I entered Dunkirk harbour at 06.00 and secured alongside the pier ahead of a destroyer and astern of trawlers. There was a sunken yacht outside the pier at the end, and a sunken trawler astern of the destroyer. The pier had been badly damaged by bombs and shell fire. Opposite the ship a gap was bridged by a brow and nearby was the body of a British soldier, killed presumably while embarking, A naval shore party consisting of two officers and some ratings were directing the troops to the various ships alongside. At the time of going alongside British troops were being directed into the destroyer astern.

Up till now things had been peaceful but at 06.17 a whistling noise was heard and the sound of an explosion, followed rapidly by about ten more. I saw from the bridge a mass of black fragments leap up on the fo'c'sle between the feet of Sub Lt N.A. Williams RNVR, my Gunnery Officer, who was at his action station alongside the 12 pounder gun on the starboard side of the fo'c'sle. The other explosions occurred very close to the ship, following rapidly one upon the other. At first the idea in everyone's mind was that these were caused by bombs, but no aeroplane was seen. When the explosions ceased a hole was found in the fo'c'sle and I was informed that a shell had burst inside the ship on the stokers' mess deck, killing five soldiers and wounding seven. Surgeon Lt Schofield RNVR immediately proceeded to the scene and the wounded were taken aft and cared for. Two were subsequently transferred to the destroyer before she sailed. The dead were laid out where they fell and were covered with blankets; they belonged to the Cheshire Regiment. Sub Lt Williams's escape was miraculous, the shell having pierced the deck exactly between his feet. I proceeded later to the mess deck, which was a shambles of blood and brains. The structural damage was not extensive, though the deck below had been pierced by fragments which included the fuse. An Artillery Officer identified the fragments as those of a 4.2 long range howitzer.

Thereafter the ship was subjected to periodic bombardment at intervals of about 20 minutes. The road to the eastward by which troops were approaching was also bombarded as were buildings in the town, apparently by the same gun or guns.

The period of waiting under bombardment was very trying for one realised that the ship might well be hit again and more loss of life bound to ensue owing to the crowds of troops on board. All officers and ratings preserved an admirable sangfroid and cheerfulness, and the troops accepted the situation with calmness. My feelings, however, and those of everyone else were that it would undoubtedly be a good thing when we were full up and could leave this decidedly unhealthy spot. Though shells fell all around the ship, some bursting practically alongside, no more hits were registered. Some fragments fell on the sweep deck aft but caused no structural damage.

The destroyer astern completed embarkation and left at 06.50 and we naturally expected to be filled up next, but this was not to be. We could see troops advancing in large numbers by the road, but they were directed to the two-funnelled channel steamer at the head of the pier. Worse still, four motor craft arrived alongside us and started taking away some of the troops already on board, but that was discouraged and we only lost about 50 in this way. By this time the tide was running in strongly and I decided to take advantage of this to turn the ship around and to occupy the billet vacated by the destroyer so that we were pointed ready for our departure. We commenced the operation at 07.00 and were bombarded whilst swinging, but again miraculously avoided being hit.

At 08.10 troops at last started coming aboard, including 13 wounded stretcher cases. A final bombardment from the howitzers occurred at this time, shells as usual falling very close. At 08.22 a German plane appeared, diving low, but was driven off by Lewis gun fire. By 08.31 I judged that we were as full as the safety of the ship permitted and I prepared to sail, but just before casting off a solitary, elderly Colonel of Ordnance appeared, footsore and weary but indubitably cheerful, shouldering an anti-tank rifle. We took him aboard, and at 08.36, with a sigh of relief, I gave the orders to slip and we proceeded for Harwich.

At 08.50 Spitfires were seen in some number which gave us a comfortable feeling. The ship was crammed with soldiers, all available space below being taken up, and the upper deck swarming as well. The troops, having eaten and drunk, mostly slept all the way.

The voyage back was uneventful. Large numbers of craft of every description passed in the opposite direction, bound for Dunkirk. The ship arrived alongside Parkeston Quay at 17.15 and disembarkation proceeded promptly. The dead were removed later in the evening.

The ship was in a shocking state of mud, wet coal dust, sand, and rubbish etc., but the military authorities sent a party on board to clean up and as soon as possible the ship was put out of routine, all hands were sent to the canteen to feed, and the stokers, whose mess deck was uninhabitable, were provided with accommodation ashore. A guard was put on the ship and everyone else retired to sleep the sleep of the just, having had none at all on the previous night.

Aboard HMS Glen Gower *on the way from Dunkirk to Harwich on Friday 31 May 1940.* (Eric Rees)

Above, below and opposite above: *Aboard HMS* Glen Gower *on the way from Dunkirk to Harwich on Friday 31 May 1940.* (Eric Rees)

Shortly after 17.00 on Friday 31 May 1940, HMS Glen Gower *arrives at Harwich after her nine hour crossing from Dunkirk. Her foredeck had been cleared of troops after it had been penetrated by a long-range enemy shell.* (Chris Collard Collection)

On 1 June 1940 the ships of the 8th Minesweeping Flotilla were ordered to proceed at 14.00 for a second trip, this time to the beaches just east of Dunkirk. On this occasion boats were taken in tow – Glen Gower having a motor boat belonging to HMS Gallant, and two cutters and a pinnace from Shotley.

The ships proceeded independently, Glen Gower leaving at 14.30. The voyage over was uneventful except for the usual alarms for aircraft. At 18.55 heavy firing could be heard to the southward. At 19.30 Spitfires and British bombers were seen, the Spitfires going homeward; while some bombers were doing the same, others were proceeding to France.

At 21.23 the fires could be seen blazing furiously at Dunkirk. Flashes of gunfire could also be seen. At 21.50 two new wrecks were passed, a large vessel on her side still burning, and a vessel close by with two funnels and a mast out of the water, afterwards known to be the wreck of HMS Brighton Queen of the 7th Minesweeping Flotilla.

Dunkirk and environs now appeared an inferno. Huge flames were shooting up from the fires in the town and the noise of gunfire and of bursting shells was terrific. At 22.45 just after passing Dunkirk a very heavy explosion took place astern which seemed to lift the ship out of the water. Looking aft we saw a big column of water go up around a small coaster which we had passed some time previously. When this had subsided the vessel had disappeared. The explosion was obviously due to a magnetic mine which we had fortunately missed.

At 22.50 a motor torpedo boat hailed us and I was told that I was now in the correct position to go inshore and anchor, which I did in four fathoms at 23.55. From now on we were continually under fire from what appeared to be 5.9in. shrapnel which was spraying the beaches and the ships. Shells were continually bursting overhead but the ship was very lucky and was hit only occasionally by pieces of shrapnel which did no damage. Occasionally another type of shell of the 'whizz bang' variety arrived on the scene. These appeared to burst in the water, shaking the ship considerably. I understand, however, that there were a good many casualties among the troops on the beach. At first the inclination of most of us was to lie down flat when the shells burst but very soon we grew accustomed to being under this form of fire and ceased to worry about it.

I had hoped to be able to lay out a kedge ashore and keep the stern towards the beach, running grasses to the shore by which the boats could pull themselves back.

This was, however, impracticable owing to the distance involved, and I could not anchor closer owing to the falling tide. The two ship's boats were therefore sent in under oars with a shore party under the charge of Lt Chapman RNVR to work in liaison with the soldiers. Instructions were to obtain a party of soldiers to surround each boat as it filled, and keep it afloat on the rapidly falling tide by pushing it out gradually. This scheme worked admirably, the soldiers being regulars of better quality than the first; no boats were left aground except the pinnace. One cutter had to be cut adrift as it was found to be waterlogged. This left the motor boat and one cutter in addition to the ship's boats.

At 02.10 the MTB hailed us to proceed at 03.00. I embarked as many troops as possible, collected the shore party and hoisted the ship's boats, taking the remaining cutter and the motor boat in tow.

I weighed anchor and proceeded at 03.20. As daylight approached we kept a wary eye open for dive bombers but none appeared, to our relief. We had about 500 troops aboard and from what we heard there were still about 2000/4000 left. I presume we were ordered to leave at

03.00 with the idea of getting away with what soldiers we had, rather than risk the certainty of being bombed at anchor and sunk with heavy loss of life. We were the last vessel to leave from our vicinity.

The embarkation on this occasion was a very trying period, in what was undoubtedly a very hot corner. Sight and hearing were almost overwhelmed by the ruddy glow of flames, the flashes of gunfire, the shrieking of shells all around and the noise of their explosions as they burst. It says much for everybody that the work was carried out calmly and steadily.

The *Glen Avon* and *Snaefell* also left the beach at just after 03.00 on Sunday 2 June, to return in company with the *Glen Gower* to Harwich. At 04.15 the *Snaefell* overtook a small, fully laden craft heading for the English coast under the command of Lt T. Ponsonby RNVR. This officer, considering that his services would be more useful at the Dunkirk beaches, returned, having transferred the troops he had rescued to the *Snaefell*.

At 04.30 the *Glen Avon* stopped off the West Buoy to pick up three Frenchmen and twenty-four Spaniards from a lifeboat bearing the name of the Dutch steamer, *Alphacca*. It appears that these men were not evacuees as they were searched, put under arrest and had their boat sunk; neither had they been shipwrecked – the *Alphacca* was, in fact, sunk on 4 April 1942. The exact circumstances surrounding this incident are not recorded. Shortly after this occurrence the *Glen Avon* drew alongside the *Glen Gower* and took aboard an army doctor to tend one of her badly injured troops who, however, later died of his wounds.

Cdr Biddulph's report continues:

On both occasions of embarkation the soldiers were very wet from wading to the boats, and our officers and ship's company were indefatigable in collecting their clothes to dry in the engine room and boiler room, lending them dry clothing and woollens in the meantime. The wardroom, at one time, presented the appearance of a Roman feast, with military officers garbed in togas from the curtains, with an undergarment of blanket around the waist.

We had a Brigadier aboard who, on arrival in harbour at 11.35, somewhat embarrassingly but very kindly called for three cheers for 'The Captain, officers and men of HMS Glen Gower *who have rescued us in our hour of peril'. We responded with three more for him and his men.*

The work of disembarkation was soon completed. We were all very weary but happy to think that we had managed to bring back some 1300 men of the BEF, and proud to know we have been able to assist in the greatest evacuation in history.

The *Glen Gower* was officially credited with the removal of 1,235 troops, the *Snaefell* with 981 and the *Glen Avon* with 888.

The three ships left Harwich, in convoy, between 10.00 and 10.30 on Wednesday 5 June and arrived at the Union Quay, North Shields, on the following day.

HMS Glen Avon *at anchor in Harwich Harbour, awaiting her return to the River Tyne, after completing two successful round trips to Dunkirk.* (Ken Jenkins Collection)

HMS Plinlimmon *at Dunkirk on the afternoon of Friday 31 May 1940. A photograph taken from the bridge of HMS* Westward Ho *by her second-in-command – the former P&A Campbell master, Lt Horace Rumsam.* (Ken Jenkins Collection)

HMS *Plinlimmon*

Under the command of Lt G.P. Baker, the *Plinlimmon* sailed from Harwich at 04.55 on Friday 31 May, and at 12.25 arrived off La Panne, where she immediately embarked thirty soldiers from a disabled motor boat. She then proceeded to Dunkirk harbour, berthing at the east mole at 14.15, and embarked about 900 troops. At 17.55, shortly after her departure, a German Messerschmidt was shot down and dived into the sea about a mile off her starboard beam. A pilot was seen coming down by parachute a short distance ahead; he landed in the water about 300 yards on the starboard bow, the ship was manoeuvred alongside and the pilot was hauled aboard. He was Plt-Off. Verity of Biggin Hill; it was he who was responsible for bringing down the enemy plane but at the same time his own aircraft was shot down by another Messerschmidt!

The *Plinlimmon* arrived at Margate at 21.00 and was ordered to return to Dunkirk on the following morning. Lt Baker's report states:

> On proceeding at 11.15 on Saturday 1 June I was ordered, by visual signal, to stop. It transpired that the Plinlimmon had not been degaussed and she was therefore debarred from taking any further part in the evacuation.
>
> We lay at anchor in Margate Roads until 09.00 on Monday 3 June when an officer came aboard and asked if I would take my entire ship's company over to HMS Oriole. I instantly assented.

HMS *Oriole* had reached Margate early on the morning of Monday 3 June after her fourth crossing from Dunkirk; the members of her crew were exhausted! After disembarking some 750 evacuees the *Oriole* moved out to the *Plinlimmon*'s anchorage, moored alongside her and the two ship's companies changed places.

The *Oriole* then made one further crossing, bringing back about fifty troops and towing two disabled motor boats; her departure from the beach at 02.20 on Tuesday 4 June making her one of the last ships to leave.

The *Plinlimmon*'s Chief Steward was Ron Gray. He and his brother Syd were long serving employees of P&A Campbell's catering department. Ron Gray recalls that aboard the *Oriole*, on her final crossing to England, 'were many of the army's top brass. I can still remember them. They were in the wardroom poring over maps while my boys were tending to their wants – grub and whisky!'

After the *Oriole*'s arrival at Margate at 13.05 the two ship's companies changed back to their original vessels. The *Plinlimmon* then made her way to Harwich before leaving for Granton at 06.55 on Wednesday 5 June.

HMS *Westward Ho*

The *Westward Ho* arrived off La Panne on the morning of Friday 31 May 1940 and immediately began to embark troops from the beach. About 150 men had been taken aboard when she was ordered to cease loading and beach herself as far inland as possible for use as an embarking stage. As already stated, this order was very soon rescinded in favour of the

Devonia. The *Westward Ho* was then ordered to proceed to Dunkirk harbour where she embarked a further 752 men, landing them at Margate later that day after a relatively uneventful round trip. It was her second journey, beginning on the following morning, which was to bring her very close to disaster!

On Saturday 1 June she arrived off Dunkirk at 14.00 and was ordered to proceed through the outer harbour and lock entrance into the inner harbour. There she embarked 900 Frenchmen, including a General and his staff. As she cast off at 16.00 the harbour was attacked by a wave of twelve enemy bombers. Although she was not directly hit, several near misses caused extensive damage to her hull; the main deck port alleyway filled with water and she began to list. Her commander, Lt A.L. Braithwaite, immediately ordered the troops to move as far to the starboard side as they could in order to lift the port sponson out of the water and to keep her on an even keel. Her steering was adversely affected and with extreme difficulty she was manoeuvred very slowly out of the crowded harbour. All the while the bombing continued and then, to add to the chaos, she was strafed by machine-gun fire which killed six and wounded twenty-one of her complement. Her two Lewis guns were continuously manned during the attack by Petty Officer Wilcox and Ordinary Seaman Banner, who were responsible for bringing down three of the aircraft. Lt Braithwaite's report states: 'It was a miracle we escaped at all.' With her leaking hull temporarily plugged, she limped across the channel to berth at Margate at 20.00. Immediately upon her arrival Petty Officer Wilcox and Ordinary Seaman Banner were decorated with the Croix de Guerre by the French General!

A signal was issued by the Flag Officer in Charge at Dover on the morning of Sunday 2 June which stated, 'Paddle minesweepers – all available are required to take part in final evacuation tonight.'

The *Westward Ho* underwent urgent repairs to her hull, and in response to this signal, was ordered to make another crossing. By the time she arrived off Dunkirk at 23.00 less than 4,000 men of the BEF remained, but conditions in the harbour were more chaotic than ever. Ships were entering, picking up whatever troops they could and leaving as quickly as possible. The longer they remained, the greater the risk of falling victim to the fury of the enemy attack.

At 02.00 on Monday 3 June, as the *Westward Ho* lay off the harbour entrance, the War Department motor cruiser, *Haig*, ferrying thirty-nine men out to the waiting ships, was struck by a French trawler and then by a French tug. The *Westward Ho* manoeuvred alongside her to embark her occupants, which included the French Naval Attaché, a number of French troops and a British Flag Commander. Despite the fact that the motor cruiser was beginning to sink, a delay was caused by an argument among some of the French troops, who appeared to be reluctant to board the paddle steamer. Meanwhile, the *Westward Ho* was moving slowly forward with the flow of the tide and became dangerously close to a nearby destroyer. Lt Braithwaite gave a 'kick astern' with the engines in order to keep clear, the wash from the paddles pushing the *Haig* a short distance away. The argument between the Frenchmen having been settled, the motor boat came alongside again and its occupants embarked. The Flag Commander immediately stormed on to the bridge and soundly abused Lt Braithwaite, accusing him of trying to murder him by attempting to sink the *Haig* with the wash from the paddles. Lt Braithwaite's report of the incident concludes by stating: 'I submit that, as the motor boat came alongside and I embarked all those on board, they were not endangered.' Nothing more was heard of the matter.

The *Westward Ho* was then ordered to leave and, despite carrying only forty-eight evacuees on her final trip, holds the record among the White Funnel steamers for bringing home the greatest number of troops – 1,686. She was also one of the luckiest ships which took part in the evacuation. She had been spared the ignominy of being beached, and had miraculously escaped from harbour under a furious enemy attack, but her third stroke of good fortune was perhaps the most remarkable – she had not fallen victim to the profusion of magnetic mines which littered the English Channel. Ironically, only after her arrival at Margate on Monday 3 June, after three crossings, was it discovered that, like the *Plinlimmon*, she had not been degaussed!

A Successful Conclusion

The signal officially starting 'Operation Dynamo' was issued by the Admiralty at 18.57 on Sunday 26 May 1940. At 14.23 on Tuesday 4 June the Admiralty announced that the operation had been completed. It had been responsible for the safe return to Great Britain of an overwhelming total of 338,226 troops. The Admiralty's statement, issued only a few hours after the final disembarkation of troops, included the following:

> The most extensive and difficult combined operation in naval history has been carried out during the past week. [...] It was undertaken on the British side by several flotillas of destroyers and a large number of craft of every description. This force rapidly increased and a total of 222 British naval vessels and 665 other British craft took part. [...] The order for the assembly of these vessels met with instantaneous response. The Admiralty cannot speak too highly of the service of all concerned. They were essential to the success of the operation and the means of saving thousands of lives.

In their reports to the Admiralty the commanders of the White Funnel steamers brought to the attention of their Lordships the names of certain individuals whose outstanding actions were of particular merit.

Acting Commander Biddulph commended:

Lt Frank Brett, Commander of HMS *Snaefell*
By skillful seamanship he successfully towed the Glen Gower *into deep water as she lay aground, and saved her from the consequences of being left behind and stranded at the mercy of enemy dive bombers.*

Lt Lachlan Shedden RNR, Navigating Officer of HMS *Glen Gower*
He relieved me of many of the cares of navigation, being, as always, utterly efficient and trustworthy, and allowed me to give more time to the general direction and supervision of preparations while under way. While at anchor, and beached, he was untiring and devoted in helping with embarking the troops, seeming to be everywhere at once.

Lt (Engineer) Eric A. Rees RNR, Chief Engineer of HMS *Glen Gower*
A pattern of cheery courage. When his duties did not keep him in the engine room he was

continually on deck assisting troops out of the boats, organising parties to assist the ship's company, and making himself generally useful. He appeared quite unmoved by the Howitzer fire and his example was undoubtedly an inspiration to others.

Sub-Lt N.A. Williams RNVR, Gunnery Officer of HMS *Glen Gower*

Organised the defence of the ship with what little remaining hands he had during embarkation and showed an example of courage and coolness when narrowly missed by the 4.2 Howitzer shell.

J. Fleming RN, Able Seaman HMS *Glen Gower*

Coxswain of one of the lifeboats on the second night. Took most excellent charge of his boat under fire and made repeated successful trips to and from the beaches, maintaining order and showing himself fully worthy of the higher rating for which he is being recommended.

L. Travers RN, Able Seaman HMS *Glen Gower*

Coxswain of a boat on both nights. On the second night he showed himself utterly fearless and was an example to all of his crew by cracking jokes as shells burst nearby, and pretending to knock them away with a piece of wood.

Acting Commander Biddulph was awarded the Distinguished Service Cross; J. Fleming was promoted to Leading Seaman and was awarded the Distinguished Service Medal.

Lt Braithwaite's report stated:

I have the honour to submit the names of the officers and men of the Westward Ho *whose conduct was outstanding during the evacuation, observing that I feel some unfairness is inevitable, when the conduct of the entire ship's company was of such high order:*

Sub-Lt (Engineer) Clifford Bohin RNR.

Showed great devotion to duty in remaining at the engine room controls and manning the engines as required, though he had been hit by a bullet.

Thomas Hussel. Able Seaman.

Showed great coolness at the helm during the heavy bombing and machine-gun attack when steering conditions were most difficult.

All of the commanders were unstinting in their praise of their entire ships' companies. Their feelings were eloquently summed up by Acting Commander Biddulph who ended his report by stating:

I would like to place upon record for the favourable notice of their Lordships the conduct of the officers and men [...] all of whom conducted themselves so admirably, with a coolness, courage, skill and energy in accordance with the highest traditions of the service.

I am proud to command such officers and men.

Wednesday, June 5, 1940   THE DAILY MIRROR   Page 3

4,000 Died Rather Than Surrender in CALAIS

One thousand British craft evacuated 335,000 Allied troops from Flanders. Allied losses in the battle were 30,000 dead, wounded or missing. The R.A.F. inflicted four-to-one losses on the German Air Force.

335,000 Saved— 30,000 Lost

Heavy losses were inflicted on the enemy on the land, but against this the Allies lost 1,000 guns, all our transport and all our armoured vehicles sent to Flanders.

The French used 500 naval and merchant ships in the evacuation, lost seven destroyers and one supply ship.

Britain previously announced the loss of six destroyers and twenty-four minor war vessels.

THE epic story of 4,000 dauntless men who held Calais to the last, spurning surrender, was told in the House of Commons yesterday.

Of those 4,000 gallant British and French troops only thirty were rescued unwounded. So far as is known, the rest fought grimly to the death.

But they had done their job; a big job. They had stemmed the German drive to Dunkirk and saved the lives of thousands of comrades.

They had written a page—as glorious a page as any yet written—in the history of the Allied struggles in defence of freedom.

Swept Like Scythe

Mr. Churchill told how German units swept like a sharp scythe, aiming at the Allies in the north.

"This armoured stroke almost reached Dunkirk—almost—but not quite," Mr. Churchill said.

"Boulogne and Calais were the scene of desperate fighting. The guards defended Boulogne for a while and were then withdrawn by orders from this country.

"The Rifle Brigade, the 60th Rifles and the Queen Victoria's Rifles—with a battalion of British tanks and a thousand Frenchmen—in all about 4,000 strong—defended Calais to the last.

"The British command" was given an hour to surrender. He spurned the offer, and four days of intense fighting passed before a silence reigned over Calais.

"Only thirty unwounded survivors were brought off by the Navy and we do not know the fate of their comrades. Their sacrifice was not however, in vain.

"At least two armoured divisions which otherwise would have been turned against the British Expeditionary force had to be sent for to overcome them.

Mostly London Men

They have added another page to the glory of the Light Division, the time gained enabled the Gravelines water-line to be held by the French troops. Thus it was that the port of Dunkirk was kept open.

The 60th Rifles, Rifle Brigade and the Queen Victoria's Rifles are recruited almost entirely from London men.

Queen Victoria's Rifles (Territorial battalions of the King's Royal Rifle Corps) came into being 137 years ago as the "Duke of Cumberland's Sharpshooters."

No other unit of the Territorial Army, save the H.A.C. possesses a continuous link so far back.

The regiment won the first V.C. ever given to a member of the Territorial Force.

The Rifle Brigade, formed as an experiment in 1800, serve, under Nelson at sea in the battle at Copenhagen, took part in the Battle of Corunna (a name which has won no significance in this war), and, under Wellington, they fired the first shots at Waterloo.

The 60th Rifles was raised in America in 1755 and for many years bore the title "The Royal Americans."

The Royal Tank Regiment is an offspring of the last war, when in the later stages its units achieved great feats of arms. Its motto is "Fear Naught."

Entente Cordiale . . . British officer hands a pie to a French soldier at a London rail terminus.

Lying on the sea bottom off Dunkirk is the Brighton Belle—pleasure steamer known to thousands. She was hit by an enemy raider. . . . One of twenty-four small vessels lost in the epic evacuation.

This Miracle Saved Our Armies from DUNKIRK

THE Premier told Parliament yesterday of how the Allied Armies had been saved by "a miracle of deliverance" from the colossal disaster of the Battle of Flanders.

A week ago, what he warned the country to expect bad and heavy tidings he feared only 20,000 men might be re-embarked.

Instead, the thousand ships carried over 335,000 Allied troops out of the jaws of death.

Mr. Churchill opened his speech by saying:

"From the moment that the French defences at Sedan and (2) the Meuse were broken at the end of the second week of May only a rapid retreat to Amiens and the south could have saved the British and French armies who had entered Belgium at the appeal of the Belgian King.

Plan Not Realised

"But this strategical plan was not immediately realised. The French High Command hoped they would be able to close the gap and the armies of the north were under their orders.

"Moreover the retirement of this kind would have involved almost certainly the destruction of the fine Belgian Army of over twenty divisions and the abandonment of the whole of Belgium.

"Therefore when the force and scene of the German penetration was realised and when the new French Generalissimo General Weygand, assumed command in place of General Gamelin, an effort was made by the French and British Armies in Belgium to keep on holding the right hand of the Belgians and to give their own right hand to the newly-created French Army which was to have advanced across the Somme in great strength to clasp it.

Communications Cut

"The German units, however, swept like a sharp scythe aiming at our Armies of the north.

"They consisted of eight or nine armoured divisions each of about 400 armoured vehicles of different kinds.

"This force cut off all communications between us and the main French Army.

"It severed our communications for food and munitions which ran first to Amiens and afterwards to Abbeville and turned its way up the coast.

"Behind this armoured and mechanised onslaught came German divisions and lorries, and behind again came plodding the dull brute mass of the German Army, always so ready to be led to the trampling down of and other land which has the liberty and comfort that they have never known in their own.

Writing home the good news two French soldiers in London yesterday—one using the other's back as a table while he "parks" his cake in his mouth.

This armoured scythe stroke at most reached Dunkirk—almost—but not quite.

Boulogne and Calais were the scene of desperate fighting—and thus it was that the port of Dunkirk was kept open.

When it was found impossible for the armies of the north to reopen their communications through Amiens with the main French armies only one test remained.

"It seemed indeed forlorn. The Belgian, British and French armies were almost surrounded; their sole line of retreat was through a single port and through its neighbouring beaches.

"They were pressed on every side by heavy attacks and far outnumbered in the air.

"When a week ago today I asked the House to fix this afternoon as the occasion for a statement. I feared it would be my hard lot to announce the greatest military disaster in our long history.

"I thought and some good judges agreed with me, that perhaps 20,000 or 30,000 men might be re-embarked but it certainly seemed that the whole of the French First Army and the whole of the B.E.F. north of the Amiens-Abbeville Gap would be broken up in the open field or else have to capitulate for lack of food and ammunition.

"These were the hard and heavy tidings for which I called upon the House and the nation to prepare themselves a week ago.

"The whole root and core of the brave British Army on which we were

French Army who were still farther from the coast than we were, and it seemed impossible that any large number of Allied troops could reach the coast.

"The enemy attacked on all sides in great strength. Their main power, the power of their far more numerous Air Force, was thrown into the battle or concentrated on the beaches of Dunkirk.

"The enemy began to fire with cannon on the beaches. They sowed magnetic mines in the channels and seas and sent repeated waves of hostile aircraft, sometimes more than 100 strong, to cast their bombs on the single pier that remained, and on the sand dunes.

"U-boats, one of which was sunk, and motor launches took their toll of the vast traffic which now began.

"For four or five days an intense struggle raged. All the armoured divisions or what was left of them together with great masses of German infantry and artillery hurled themselves upon the ever narrowing and contracting appendix in which the French and British armies fought.

M.P.s Cheer Navy

Meanwhile the Royal Navy—(loud cheers)—with a navy host of merchant shipping strove every nerve to embark the troops.

"Two hundred and twenty light warships and more than 650 other vessels were employed on a difficult coast and under increasing fire.

"It was in conditions such as these that the Army carried on, with little or no rest for day or night on end.

"The ships made trip after trip always bringing out the men. The numbers brought back are the measure of their courage.

"Hospital ships brought off many thousands of wounded but, were a special target for the Nazi bombs. Nevertheless, the men and women on board never faltered in their duty.

Struggle Was Fierce

"Our Royal Air Force had been engaged in the battle throughout, and it now brought into use part of the main Metropolitan fighter strength and struck at the German fighters and bombers.

"The struggle was protracted and fierce. Suddenly the scene has cleared.

"The crash and thunder has for the moment—and I say for the moment—died away.

"A miracle of deliverance has been achieved by the valour, per-

(Continued on Page 14.)

"That was the prospect a week ago.

But another blow which might well have proved final was yet to fall upon us."

Mr. Churchill recalled that it was the Allies who rescued Belgium from extinction in the late war.

"Had not this ruler sought refuge in what has proved to be a fatal neutrality, the French and British armies might well at the very outset have saved not only Belgium, but perhaps even Holland.

"Yet at the last moment," Mr. Churchill added, "when Belgium was already invaded, King Leopold called upon us to come to his aid, and even at the last moment we came.

"His brave and efficient army, nearly half a million strong, was on our Eastern flank and was upon our line of retreat to the sea.

"Suddenly, without prior consultation, with the least possible notice, upon his own personal act, he sent a plenipotentiary to the German Command surrendering his army and exposing our whole flank without the means of retreat (Cries of "Shame")

"Treachery"

"I asked the House a week ago to suspend judgment because the facts were not clear.

"But I do not feel that any reason now exists why we should not form our own opinion upon this pitiful episode. (Cheers and shouts of "Treachery.")

"The surrender of the Belgian Army compelled the British at the shortest notice to cover a flank to the sea more than 300 miles in length, otherwise they would have been cut off and all would have shared the fate to which King Leopold had condemned the finest army his country had ever formed.

"In doing this he closed his flank.

"Contact was lost inevitably between the British and two out of the three corps forming the First

On the day following the successful conclusion of 'Operation Dynamo' the above article appeared in the Daily Mirror. *The caption beneath the* Brighton Belle *photograph is inaccurate regarding the position and cause of her sinking.*

Business as Usual

Of course, whatever happens at Dunkirk we shall fight on.

Parliament assembled on Tuesday 4 June 1940 and was told by Winston Churchill, Prime Minister since Neville Chamberlain resigned on 10 May after the failure of the Norwegian campaign, 'We must be very careful not to assign to this deliverance the attributes of victory. Wars are not won by evacuations.' In his history of the Second World War he states:

> There was of course a darker side to Dunkirk. We had lost the whole equipment of the army to which all the first-fruits of our factories had hitherto been given. Many months must elapse, even if the existing programmes were fulfilled without interruption by the enemy, before this loss could be repaired. [...]
>
> The troops returned with nothing but rifles and bayonets and a few hundred machine-guns, and were forthwith sent to their homes for seven days' leave. Their joy at being once again united with their families did not overcome a stern desire to engage the enemy at the earliest moment. [...] Their morale was high, and they rejoined their regiments and batteries with alacrity.

The surviving steamers of the White Funnel Fleet returned to their bases to resume their minesweeping duties – the *Plinlimmon*, *Skiddaw* and *Westward Ho* to Granton; the *Glen Gower*, *Glen Avon* and *Snaefell* rejoining the *Glen Usk* on the Tyne.

Two weeks after the Dunkirk evacuation P&A Campbell received a letter from the Ministry of Shipping which stated:

> I am directed by the Minister of Shipping to inform you that it was with great regret that he learned from the Admiralty of the loss of the *Brighton Queen* and the *Brighton Belle*. He also understands that the *Devonia* must be regarded as a total loss.

The claims for compensation for the three steamers were set in motion but were not settled until over two years later.

We must retrace our steps at this point to the General Meeting of P& A Campbell Ltd held in Bristol on Thursday 16 May 1940.

The Chairman stated that the Admiralty had granted permission for the continuation of the Cardiff to Weston ferry with one steamer, the *Ravenswood*. This was to be a restricted service which, owing to the possibility of night air raids, would operate only between the hours of sunrise and sunset. The Chairman added that whether or not it would be a success was impossible to say, but the company felt it was their duty to the public to try it out. If it proved unprofitable or undesirable in any way it would be brought to an end.

Mr Keen had written to Mr Allen, on 22 April 1940:

The Ravenswood, *the only paddler now in Bristol, has just come out of dry-dock and is fitting out for the Cardiff-Weston ferry. She is expected to take a good deal of money this summer, especially as the air ferry between the two towns has now been discontinued.*

A few weeks later Mr Allen wrote in reply:

The Ravenswood *sailed on the morning of Friday 10 May from Bristol to Cardiff, to start the ferry on the following day. As with the* Duchess of Devonshire *in the last war, she is manned by those personnel unfit for naval service. Capt. William Riddell is in command, with Capt. William Bruford as mate and Chief Officer Jimmy Martin as bosun.*

I understand that permission was granted for the service provided that the Ravenswood *is available to take on tendering duties instantly the call for this work is made. I gather she is to serve, if necessary, as a tender to hospital ships, and will therefore probably carry a red cross on her white funnel.*

At the board meeting in mid-June it was stated by the Managing Director, Mr William James Banks, that the service was not proving remunerative, but after discussion it was decided to continue the sailings for the time being.

A correspondent of the writer, Mr William Widden, recalls a brief but significant memory of the early summer of 1940:

On one occasion my wife wanted to visit friends in Cheddar. We lived in Swansea at the time but learned that the Ravenswood *was still operating the Cardiff to Weston ferry and decided to avail ourselves of that pleasure.*

It proved to be the day the first bombs had fallen on Cardiff, overturning a couple of coal trucks at the docks. We didn't know anything about this until we stepped off the tram at the Pier Head and saw the Western Mail *placard – 'Cardiff bombed'. We looked at each other, shrugged our shoulders and made straight for the pontoon.*

There was the dear old Ravenswood, *but with a difference! Her lifeboats were slung outboard and hatchets hung from the davits. There were not many passengers, but she sailed on time on both the outward and homeward journeys.*

Walking down the gangway back at Cardiff, we later found that we had both had the same thought – may she come safely through her second world war.

Mr Widden states that 'There were not many passengers...' – an all too frequent occurrence which was to bring about the end of the service. The minutes of the board meeting of Friday 12 July state that because of the danger from intermittent daylight air attacks and the consequent lack of passengers, sailings after her final crossing from Weston to Cardiff on Wednesday 3 July had been discontinued. On the following day she left Cardiff at 05.00 and arrived at Bristol at 07.00, finally berthing in the Merchant's Dock at 10.30, having been delayed between 08.00 and 09.30 by an air raid.

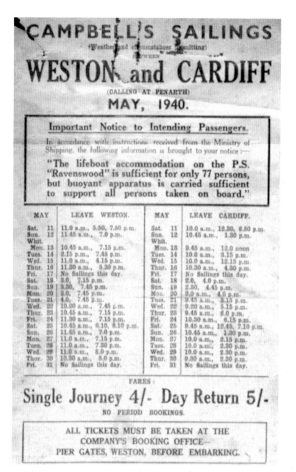

CAMPBELL'S SAILINGS

(Weather and circumstances permitting)

WESTON and CARDIFF

(CALLING AT PENARTH)

MAY, 1940.

Important Notice to Intending Passengers.

In accordance with instructions received from the Ministry of Shipping, the following information is brought to your notice :—

"The lifeboat accommodation on the P.S. "Ravenswood" is sufficient for only 77 persons, but buoyant apparatus is carried sufficient to support all persons taken on board."

MAY	LEAVE WESTON.	MAY	LEAVE CARDIFF.
Sat. 11	11.0 a.m., 5.50, 7.50 p.m.	Sat. 11	10.0 a.m., 12.30, 6.50 p.m.
Sun. 12	11.45 a.m., 7.0 p.m.	Sun. 12	10.45 a.m., 1.30 p.m.
Whit.		Whit.	
Mon. 13	10.45 a.m., 7.15 p.m.	Mon. 13	9.45 a.m., 12.0 noon
Tues. 14	2.15 p.m., 7.45 p.m.	Tues. 14	10.0 a.m., 3.15 p.m.
Wed. 15	11.0 a.m., 4.15 p.m.	Wed. 15	10.0 a.m., 12.15 p.m.
Thur. 16	11.30 a.m., 5.30 p.m.	Thur. 16	10.30 a.m., 4.30 p.m.
Fri. 17	No Sailings this day.	Fri. 17	No Sailings this day.
Sat. 18	3.0, 7.15 p.m.	Sat. 18	2.0, 4.0 p.m.
Sun. 19	3.30, 7.45 p.m.	Sun. 19	2.30, 4.45 p.m.
Mon. 20	3.0, 7.45 p.m.	Mon. 20	3.0 a.m., 4.0 p.m.
Tues. 21	4.0, 7.45 p.m.	Tues. 21	9.45 a.m., 5.15 p.m.
Wed. 22	10.30 a.m., 7.45 p.m.	Wed. 22	9.20 a.m., 5.15 p.m.
Thur. 23	10.45 a.m., 7.15 p.m.	Thur. 23	9.45 a.m., 6.0 p.m.
Fri. 24	11.30 a.m., 7.15 p.m.	Fri. 24	10.30 a.m., 6.15 p.m.
Sat. 25	10.45 a.m., 6.10, 8.10 p.m.	Sat. 25	9.45 a.m., 12.45, 7.10 p.m.
Sun. 26	11.45 a.m., 7.0 p.m.	Sun. 26	10.45 a.m., 1.30 p.m.
Mon. 27	11.0 a.m., 7.15 p.m.	Mon. 27	10.0 a.m., 2.15 p.m.
Tues. 28	11.0 a.m., 7.30 p.m.	Tues. 28	10.0 a.m., 2.30 p.m.
Wed. 29	11.0 a.m., 8.0 p.m.	Wed. 29	10.0 a.m., 2.30 p.m.
Thur. 30	10.30 a.m., 5.0 p.m.	Thur. 30	9.30 a.m., 2.30 p.m.
Fri. 31	No Sailings this day.	Fri. 31	No Sailings this day.

FARES :

Single Journey 4/- Day Return 5/-

NO PERIOD BOOKINGS.

ALL TICKETS MUST BE TAKEN AT THE COMPANY'S BOOKING OFFICE— PIER GATES, WESTON, BEFORE EMBARKING.

One of the timetables of the Ravenswood's ferry sailings for the curtailed season of 1940.

The withdrawal of the *Ravenswood* brought about a most unusual situation. Each summer, since the first White Funnel steamer, the *Waverley*, sailed from Bristol in 1887, a service of some sort had been provided. Even during the First World War the Cardiff to Weston ferry continued with the *Waverley* and *Glen Rosa* in 1915/1916, and during 1917/1918 with the *Duchess of Devonshire*, the steamer which the company chartered from the Devon Dock Pier & Steamship Co. But, in 1940, for the first summer in over fifty years, the Bristol Channel was bereft of a White Funnel steamer in operation.

On a more optimistic note, once again we must return to the General Meeting of Thursday 16 May 1940 and quote the company chairman, Mr G.H. Boucher:

> *You will remember that at our meeting last year you were informed that we had placed an order for a new ship. This ship was launched on 29 February this year and will be in commission early next month. Intimation has been given to us that she will be requisitioned by the Admiralty. She is a very fine ship and it is a great tragedy that we are unable to make use of her for the purposes for which she was built. However, she will pay for her keep and we hope that the war will soon be over and enable her to carry out the duties for which she was specially constructed.*

Mr Allen had stated, during the summer of 1939, that names under consideration for her were 'Southern Queen', 'Albion' and 'Britannia II'; 'Albion' then being the current favourite. He added, 'I am told there is not going to be any more "Hastings Belle" or "Eastbourne Queen" business.'

The launch of the turbine steamer at the Ailsa Shipbuilding Co.'s yard, Troon, on Thursday 29 February 1940. The ship was launched by Mrs Banks, who can be seen holding a bouquet of flowers. Her husband, Mr William Banks, Managing Director of P&A Campbell Ltd, is standing immediately behind the two ladies on Mrs Banks' left. The ship was named Empress Queen, *a name greeted with derision from most quarters.* (Ken Jenkins Collection)

The *Empress Queen* left Troon on the morning of Tuesday 16 April 1940, in tow of two of the Clyde Shipbuilding Co.'s tugs. She was seen passing Dunoon at 12.40 on her way to Harland & Wolff's Yard at Govan, Glasgow, for the installation of her engines.

By the end of May 1940 rumours were circulating that the new steamer would arrive at Bristol later that summer for conversion for war service. Mr Allen urged Mr Keen to photograph her 'in case anything happens to her during the course of the hostilities', but because of the wartime restrictions on photography in dockland areas, this was not going to be easy, as Mr Keen explained:

> *The* Empress Queen *is expected to come to Bristol, as you say. Captains Jack George and Bernard Hawken will go north to bring her around, but my chances of taking photographs of her are nil. Our Bristol police are very hot and no permits are being granted. I do not feel inclined to put my head in a noose however much I desire a picture.*

At the board meeting of 12 July 1940 the directors were appraised of the latest developments of the new steamer when the secretary read a letter, dated 10 July 1940, which had been received from the Ailsa Shipbuilding Co. Ltd; a part of which stated :

> *Regarding the turbine steamer* Empress Queen, *particularly with reference to the official trials of the vessel which took place on Wednesday 3 July, we take it that Mr. Banks, who was present, has reported to you that these were entirely satisfactory in every way.*
>
> *The mean speed attained under full power was 19.66 knots, which is slightly more than one eighth of a knot in excess of the contract requirements. In addition, the vessel was carrying an excess weight of about 25 tons. It was unfortunate that on the day of the trials a very strong wind was blowing which made a difference of about two knots per hour less going against the wind than with it, and it is a well known fact that what you lose in the one direction, you cannot fully recover that loss on the run in the other direction with wind and tide in favour of the ship. The shaft horsepower developed was 4140.*
>
> *For you own, and our satisfaction, might we respectfully suggest that after the vessel has been returned to us for reconditioning, and removal of the air raid precaution fittings in connection with bridge protection, a further trial might be carried out on the Arran mile as before.*
>
> *Our only regret is that the vessel was not completed in accordance with contract, as we were anxious to obtain a suitable photograph for advertising in the various shipping journals.*

Following her trials, the *Empress Queen* was held in reserve at the Ailsa Shipbuilding Co.'s yard, and did not visit Bristol as expected. She was requisitioned on 4 October 1940 but was released exactly a month later, having remained at Troon in the meantime.

Above and below: *The* Empress Queen *on trials in the Firth of Clyde. Wednesday 3 July 1940.* (C.G. Boath/Ken Jenkins Collection)

The *Empress Queen* was requisitioned again on 22 November 1940, this time with instructions for delivery to Sheerness. She was sailed around the north of Scotland to the Thames by Capt. Jack George, who reported very favourably on her sea-going qualities. At Sheerness she was refitted as an anti-aircraft vessel and, at the same time, was renamed *Queen Eagle*, before joining the Thames Special Service Flotilla. Her War Risks Insurance Valuation amounted, initially, to £155,206.

In the meantime the Campbell minesweepers went about their daily business in the North Sea. Despite the fact that all of the steamers underwent periodic refits as well as routine maintenance, frequent repairs were necessary, especially to their paddles which were so vulnerable to floating debris and the heavy seas of the winter gales. The ships of the 8th Flotilla were fortunate in that the work was carried out locally, usually at Brigham & Cowan's Yard in the Albert Edward Dock, on the Tyne. The 7th Flotilla, however, had to travel farther afield, and during October and November 1940, for example, the *Plinlimmon* was overhauled at Aberdeen and the *Westward Ho* on the Tyne. The *Skiddaw* sailed south in March 1941 for an overhaul on the Humber.

The *Glen Gower* took part in a number of notable events and incidents:

Tuesday 6 August 1940
She was one of a number of venues for a Royal visit to Tyneside when HRH Duke of Kent spent about an hour on board. (The Duke had paid a similar visit to the *Snaefell* on 8 March 1940.)

Thursday 26 September 1940
She developed engine trouble off the mouth of the Tyne and was towed into port by her flotilla consort, the New Medway Steam Packet Co.'s paddle steamer, *Thames Queen*. Some time later the *Glen Gower* performed a similar service for another member of her flotilla when she towed the General Steam Navigation Co.'s paddler, *Laguna Belle*, disabled owing to engine trouble, into the Tyne. On this occasion both vessels were harassed by enemy air attacks, but luckily sustained no damage.

Saturday 5 October 1940
She rescued the entire crew of the Dutch steamer, *Ottoland* (2,202 gross tons), which sank off Seaham. The *Ottoland*'s voyage had brought her across the north Atlantic from the Canadian port of Buctouche, with a cargo of pit props bound for Immingham. Having reached Methil, on the Firth of Forth, she joined a convoy which set off on the journey south to the Humber, but struck a stray mine in position Lat. 54°50' N, Long. 0°53' W. The *Glen Gower*, part of the minesweeping force accompanying the convoy through its section of the War Channel, was first at the scene. She steamed through a seemingly endless amount of timber, which had been washed from the *Ottoland*'s deck, before reaching the ship's lifeboats and rescuing all forty-three members of her officers and crew.

8-20 June 1941

In the summer of 1941 the *Glen Gower* underwent a change of name, made necessary by communication problems.

The Royal Naval establishment which had been opened in the spring of 1940, at Pwllheli, North Wales, had been given the name HMS Glendower. The obvious similarity between the two names caused more and more confusion, especially as the personnel at the shore base increased in number. The *Glen Gower* was therefore renamed *Glenmore*. The exact date of the change is not known but it was implemented between 8 and 20 June 1941 and remained with her for the duration of her naval service.

Aboard HMS Glen Gower, *bringing in sweeps in a North Sea gale. HMS* Glen Usk *can be seen in the distance.* (Eric Rees)

HMS Glen Gower *and HMS* Glen Usk *in line ahead, 1941.* (Eric Rees)

Waves break over the south breakwater at the entrance to the River Tyne in a force 8 gale from the north east as the Glen Gower *and, ahead of her, the* Glen Usk *wait to enter port, 1941.* (Eric Rees)

HMS Glen Gower *berthed at the Fish Quay, North Shields, in 1941.* (Eric Rees)

Above: *The Dutch cargo steamer* Ottoland *sinking off Seaham after striking a stray mine in the War Channel. Saturday 5 October 1940.* (Eric Rees)

Left: *Survivors from the* Ottoland *being taken aboard the* Glen Gower. *Saturday 5 October 1940.* (Eric Rees)

The officers and crew of HMS Glen Gower *at North Shields in 1940. Among those seated on the chairs are: Lt-Com. M.A. Biddulph (third from left); Lt Lachlan McLean Shedden (second from left); and Chief Engineer Lt (E) Eric Rees (second from right).* (Peter Southcombe Collection)

Lt-Com. Biddulph in discussion with his officers and crew on the after deck of the Glen Gower. (Eric Rees)

The 12-pounder gun on the foredeck of HMS Glen Gower. (Eric Rees)

A view from the foredeck of HMS Glen Gower, *showing the shield which was fitted to the 12-pounder shortly after the Dunkirk evacuation.* (Eric Rees)

Above and below: *Members of the crew of HMS* Snaefell. (Ken Jenkins Collection)

The ships of the 7th Flotilla were involved in a somewhat unusual sweeping operation in the Firth of Forth during the autumn of 1940. A British minefield had been laid in September 1939, by HMS *Plover*, in the vicinity of Bass Rock. The routing of the east coast convoys was constantly being changed to confuse the enemy; the thirty-two mines that remained from the original field of 146, were 'in the way', adversely affecting the flexibility of the convoy routes, and had to be removed. The mines, and their thin, single strand wire moorings dated from 1919, and it was decided that the quickest and most effective method of clearance would be, not by using Oropesa apparatus, but by using the traditional 'First World War method' of two sweepers towing a sunken wire, parallel to the seabed, between them. The *Westward Ho*, *Plinlimmon* and *Skiddaw* were detailed for the task, reminiscent of the work which they had performed so well in the previous conflict. The subsequent report from the Commander of Minesweepers at Granton stated:

> *Operations commenced on Saturday 14 September 1940 and were successfully completed on Sunday 22 September. On one day the weather was unfavourable, and another was devoted to a different and more urgent operation. Tide and light conditions restricted operations to two hours either side of high water in daylight only, and a total of 27 sweeping hours were necessary.*
>
> *The* Westward Ho, Plinlimmon *and* Skiddaw *were eminently suitable for the task, with their shallow draught, and were handled in an excellent manner by their commanding officers. Not one 'lap' had to be re-swept owing to bad handling or station keeping, and sweep passing was always done by heaving line – it reflects great credit upon the ships and personnel concerned.*

Air Attacks and Barrage Balloons

With regard to the wider issues of the conflict: early in 1940 the German Supreme Command had issued its first directive for the planning of a cross-channel invasion of Great Britain, but the German Commanders of land, sea and air became more and more opposed in their opinions as to how it should proceed. One point on which they were, however, in agreement was the necessity for superiority in the air, and in July 1940 the Luftwaffe began its massive assault on south-east England in its attempt to annihilate the Royal Air Force and its installations, and to lay waste the coastal ports designated as landing places for the forthcoming invasion. The attempt failed; the Luftwaffe, despite outnumbering the British forces, had not anticipated the outstanding bravery and daring of the RAF fighter pilots!

Intermittent air raids on London in August 1940 led to a retaliatory attack on Berlin; Hitler took full advantage of this reprisal and announced his intention of reducing London and other British cities to chaos and ruin. This marked the beginning of the 'Blitz'. Although the worst of this massive assault had ended by the spring of 1941, heavy air raids continued for over a year, when the sea ports became specific targets.

Air attacks on the minesweepers became a frequent hazard and on 15 February 1941 the *Westward Ho* engaged an enemy bomber in the Firth of Forth, but both adversaries escaped damage. The exact details of all such incidents, whether causing damage or not, had to be reported to the Admiralty via the ships' Base Commanders.

On 1 June 1941 an abortive attack was carried out in the Firth of Forth on ships of the 7th Flotilla; the report, submitted by Lt G.P. Baker of the *Plinlimmon*, included the following:

Report of Attack by Enemy Aircraft on Plinlimmon *and* Skiddaw

Position – 3 miles east of May Island.
Course – South-west. Speed 12 knots.
Weather – Overcast. Sea calm. Cloud 1500ft. Wind NE, force 2.
Visibility – 20 miles.
Particulars of attack – Low level bomber.
Number of Aircraft – One.
Type of Aircraft – Junkers 88.
Direction – 55 on port bow. 2 bombs dropped from 600ft.
Bomb Type – 500lbs, impact. Fell 4 cables on port beam.
No hits, no damage, no casualties.
Defence – Long range. 3 rounds on 12-pounder, 2 Lewis guns & 1 Hotchkiss.
Damage to Aircraft – Probably none. Range too great.
Narrative Report – At 11.55 the enemy aeroplane was seen about three miles away, about 50° on the port bow, in a steep dive. Fire was opened with machine-guns at extreme range. The two bombs were dropped simultaneously. The helm was put hard-a-starboard to bring the 12-pounder to bear. Three rounds were fired from the latter before the aeroplane was out of range. The aeroplane was seen to circle round for some moments at a distance of about five miles and was last seen proceeding in a northerly direction. When the attack commenced HMS Skiddaw *was stationed six cables off the port beam of* Plinlimmon.

Sent to Admiralty via Naval Officer in Charge, Leith and Granton.

HMS Plinlimmon *at anchor in Arbroath Bay, August 1940.* (Ron Gray)

Paddle minesweepers in line ahead. A view from the bridge of the New Medway Steam Packet Co.'s Queen of Thanet, *with the* Plinlimmon *and* Skiddaw *following her into the Firth of Forth on a summer evening in 1940.* (Horace Rumsam/Ken Jenkins Collection)

HMS Skiddaw *at anchor in Arbroath Bay, August 1940.* (Ken Jenkins Collection)

With Inchkeith Island in the background, HMS Skiddaw *explodes mines in her sweep.* (Chris Collard Collection)

Members of the crew of HMS Glen Usk *photographed in her engine room.* (Eric Rees)

GLEN USK.

Tempy. Lieut.-Com., R.N.V.R.	} N. F. Wills	8 Oct 39
Tempy. Lieut., R.N.R.	} E. C. Phillips (act)	3 Nov 39
Tempy. Lieut., R.N.V.R.	} D. W. Poulton	12 Feb 40
	J. A. Hill	9 Sept 40
	D. J. L. Adamson	4 Nov 40
Tempy. Lieut. (E), R.N.R.	} K. Jones	16 Oct 40
Tempy. Sub-Lieut. (E), R.N.R.	} G. W. Lugton	16 Oct 40
Tempy. Act. Sub-Lieut.(E) R.N.V.R.	} J. S. Mather	16 Oct 40

GLEN AVON.

Tempy. Lieut. Com., R.N.R.	} A. Stubbs (act)	2 July 40
Tempy. Lieut., R.N.R.	} A. V. Murphy	29 Nov 40
	C. R. Clark	31 Oct 39
Tempy. Lieut., R.N.V.R.	} G. H. Law	27 Jan 40
	T. H. Davies	10 Jan 41
Tempy. Lieut. (E), R.N.R.	} A. Campbell	18 Oct 39
Tempy. Act. Sub-Lieut.(E) R.N.V.R.	} R. J. Dawson	2 Nov 39
	T. G. Hicks	3 Nov 39

GLEN GOWER.

Commander, R.N.R.	} W. J. Rice, RD	17 Mar 41
Tempy. Lieut., R.N.R.	} L. M. Shedden	1 Nov 40
Tempy. Lieut., R.N.V.R.	} W. A. Cuthbertson	23 Jan 40
	N. A. F. Williams	30 Jan 40
	M. Gardner	14 Feb 41
	E. Morris	16 Feb 41
Tempy. Lieut. (E), R.N.R.	} E. A. Rees	29 Apr 40
Tempy. Surg. Lieut., R.N.V.R.	} J. V. Rose, MRCS, LRCP (proby)	6 Jan 41
Tempy. Sub-Lieut., R.N.V.R.	} E. M. Derane	17 Oct 39
	A. J. Boss (proby)	10 Jan 41
Tempy. Sub-Lieut. (E), R.N.R.	} P. C. Luck	20 Nov 39
	J. E. Burdon	8 July 40
Tempy. Paym. Sub-Lieut., R.N.V.R.	} D. G. Johnston	20 Feb 40

GLENDOWER.

(Training Establishment Pwllheli, North Wales.)

Captain	J. Figgins	1 Oct 40
Commander	F. A. Pigou (ret)	20 Nov 40
	J. M. Rogers (act)	— Feb 41
	B. F Johnson (act)	25 Feb 41
Lieut.-Com.	R. N. Fothergill	1 Oct 40
	C. T. R. Searle (ret)	1 Oct 40
	M. H. Le Mare (ret)	1 Oct 40
Lieutenant	C. M. K. Bruton	21 Feb 41
Lieutenant, R.N.R.	} W. Atkinson, MBE	3 Jan 41
Tempy. Lieut., R.N.V.R.	} K. J. Gordon (vet)	14 June 40
	D'A. M. Stephens	5 Dec 40
	A. R. Truswell	6 Nov 40
	T. McE. Porter	23 June 40
	D. Burcart	6 Nov 40
	G. B. Parry (act)	14 June 40
	S. C. Bell	6 Nov 40
	J. K. Sherwood	27 June 40
Lieutenant (E) ...	J. C. Robinson (ret)	29 Nov 40
Chaplain	Rev. N. C. Jones, BA	8 Oct 40
Tempy. Chaplain, R.N.V.R.	} Rev. W. H. Woodhouse, BA (proby)	8 Oct 40
Surg. Capt.	J. A. O'Flynn, MD	2 July 40
Paym. Capt.	C. A. Shove, OBE (ret)	1 Oct 40
Surg. Com. (D).	S. Mawer, LDS	12 Aug 40
Tempy. Surg. Lieut. Com., R.N.V.R.	} G. B. Stratton, MRCS, LRCP (proby)	15 July 40
	(S) R. A. Barlow, MB, chB	18 Feb 41
Tempy. Surg.-Lieut., R.N.V.R.	} H. V. Lavelle, MB, chB ...	— Nov 40
	R. M. M. Hunter, MB, chB, DPH (proby)	28 Aug 40
Tempy. Surg. Lieut. (D), R.N.V.R.	} E. W. King-Turner, LDS...	5 Aug 40
	P. A. Crow, LDS	1 Oct 40
	G. W. Hughes, LDS (proby)	— Nov 40
	P. C. Bisson, LDS (proby)..	18 Feb 41
Paym. Lieut.	A. T. Smart (ret)	1 Oct 40
Paym. Lieut., R.N.V.R.	} R. S. Borner, ACA	7 Oct 40
	P. W. Wood	9 Dec 40
Shipwright Lieut.	} T. H. Stonehouse (ret) ...	30 Nov 40
Wardmaster Lieut.	} E. P. Harn (ret)	1 Aug 40
Tempy. Paym. Sub-Lieut., R.N.V.R.	} G. A. Taylor	1 Oct 40
Tempy. Lieut. (Sp. Br.), R.N.V.R.	} G. G. Turner	6 Nov 40
Gunner	H. V. Ball (ret)	18 Nov 40
	A. G. Carey (ret)	28 Nov 40
Tempy. Gunner	} R. E. Lines (act)	18 Nov 40
	P. Chapman (act).	18 Nov 40
Boatswain	J. P. Nichols	6 Oct 40
	W. F. Pacey (ret).	20 Jan 41
	H. Smith (ret)	1 Feb 41
	H. E. Summers (ret)	20 Jan 41
Tempy. Boatswain	} H. N. Schorah (act)	15 July 40
Tempy. M.A.A.	} G. W. Corkett (act)	7 Dec 40
Wt. Writer	S. V. Norris	7 Jan 41
Tempy. Wt. Cook	} W. H. Turner (act)	4 Dec 40

Extracts from the 'Navy List' of March 1941. This was a confidential, quarterly publication which gave a wealth of information concerning the ships, shore establishments and personnel of the Royal Navy, Royal Naval Reserve and Royal Naval Volunteer Reserve, including the dates on which individuals joined their current commands. (Public Records Office Ref: ADM 177)

With the sun rising over the Firth of Forth, HMS Plinlimmon *heads out to sea for another day's minesweeping.* (H.G. Owen Collection)

"Any luck? Not 'arf," said the crew of the fishing trawler as they unloaded a gift for dinner to the boat of a minesweeper which spotted them, and smelled fried plaice in the offing.

A newspaper cutting showing HMS Skiddaw *in the North Sea. The caption says it all!* (Chris Collard Collection)

POPULAR SHIP WILL SAIL NO MORE

WAVERLEY LOST

BRISTOLIANS who patronise the White Funnel Fleet of pleasure steamers in peace-time will learn with regret of the loss of one of its most popular vessels—the Waverley, the wartime name of which was Snaefell.

The announcement is made by the Admiralty, who state that next of kin of casualties have been informed.

Waverley was employed mainly on the Cardiff-Weston ferry, but she was equally serviceable on any of Messrs. Campbell's runs. Waverley also recalls the days of competition from the former Barry Railway Co., some of whose vessels were eventually taken over by Messrs. Campbell's. Waverley was one of them, her name then being Barry.

So far as is known there were no Bristol people aboard at the time of the loss. It is understood that some Bristol officers who were serving on the Waverley were transferred on promotion quite recently. Waverley took a very prominent part in the Dunkirk evacuation.

In naming the vessel Waverley, Messrs. Campbell perpetuated the name of the ship with which they inaugurated their Bristol Channel enterprise.

A newspaper report of the loss of HMS Snaefell.

Although the paddle steamers experienced many narrow escapes from air attacks, tragedy struck on 5 July 1941. The *Snaefell* and *Glen Avon* were sweeping together, in company with other ships of the 8th Flotilla, in the War Channel, a few miles east of Sunderland, when they were bombed by enemy aircraft. A direct hit was scored on the *Snaefell* which sank in position Lat. 54°51' N, Long. 1°27' W. It has been impossible to trace any official reports of the incident, or to ascertain the extent of loss of life aboard the *Snaefell*. However, one of her engineers, Temporary Sub-Lt Herbert Gilbert Webster, of Milford Haven, was mentioned in Despatches after he gave up his place in a lifeboat for a wounded seaman. A newspaper later reported how Sub-Lt Webster, having left the lifeboat, swam to a life raft which he shared with one other occupant. A large number of huge cod, stunned by the bomb explosion, had risen to the surface, which the engineer proceeded to lift out of the water and place in the bottom of the raft. So busy was he that he failed to notice that his companion was equally as busy throwing them out; he complained that as they were reviving they were biting his bare feet!

In December 1941 another member of the paddle steamer personnel received an award for his gallant action. A report in the Admiralty records states:

Stoker S.G. Elvin of HM Paddle Minesweeper, Skiddaw, *who was confined to his bunk in the ship, under medical supervision, heard cries for help. Without a moment's hesitation he doubled up on deck, over the gangway and along the dock wall to a point from which the cries emanated. In total darkness with no moon and a heavy sky, Elvin dived in and eventually found Stoker Fottrell, a non-swimmer, struggling in the water. Elvin succeeded in getting him to the dockside, by which time a floodlight had been put on the water. Both rescuer and rescued were then pulled ashore. Fottrell was unconscious and needed half-an-hour of artificial respiration before being taken to hospital, where he made a complete recovery.*

For his gallant action Stoker S.G. Elvin was later presented with the Royal Humane Society's Medal by Admiral Sir C.G. Ramsay, Commander in Chief, Rosyth.

Towards the end of 1941 all of the White Funnel steamers were equipped to carry barrage balloons. Although these appendages were an important deterrent against attacking aircraft, they were ungainly and difficult to handle, even in the slightest wind, and were a frequent source of frustration to the crew. The balloon mooring wires often parted or became entangled in the rigging; the fabric of the balloon was easily torn on their crowded decks and it was not unknown for them to burst. An amusing entry in one of the *Glen Avon's* log books states: 'Barrage balloon busted – again!'

Nevertheless, the *Glen Avon's* company had good cause to be thankful for its 'inflatable monster' on the evening of 5 September 1941. While sweeping off Hartlepool, flying her balloon at 300ft, a Heinkel 111 aircraft swooped from the cloud cover and dropped five bombs. The damage report states: 'Two hits unexploded, three near misses. Minor damage to machinery and fittings.' The crew opened fire with the 12-pounder, Hotchkiss and Lewis gun, but the bomber disappeared as quickly as it had materialised. The *Glen Avon's* Commanding Officer, Acting Commander Archie Stubbs, Senior Officer of the 8th Minesweeping Flotilla, ended his report by stating:

Enemy aircraft carried out attack in skilful manner. He released bombs as he banked to miss our balloon cable by about 50ft. No machine-gun or cannon attack made, probably because pilot was concentrating on avoiding balloon wire and pilot's avoiding action was too sudden for rear gunner to take action.

Eagle Ships

Since the termination of the Cardiff to Weston ferry, in July 1940, the *Ravenswood* had remained laid up in Bristol. She presented a most unusual sight as her funnel, ventilators, and the tops of her paddle boxes had been painted black to render her less conspicuous from the air. However, she had sustained considerable fire damage to her after saloon in the first incendiary raid on the city on the night of 24 November 1940. Nevertheless, she was requisitioned on 6 August 1941; the last member of the Campbell fleet to be called up. It was originally intended to base her at Londonderry, for use in Lough Foyle, but this location was quickly changed.

The Flag Officer in Charge at Belfast had written to the Admiralty:

On account of the size of Belfast Lough and the shallow depth of water throughout, it is very vulnerable to magnetic minelaying by aircraft. The swept channel is 15 miles long. As there will always be a large number of vessels anchored in the Lough for degaussing, searching, and routeing instructions, and also as large numbers of small vessels use the Lough for shelter in bad weather, it is considered that the provision of some adequate anti-aircraft defence is necessary. Approval is required for a balloon barrage, the balloons to be flown from moored barges. This would also afford protection for the port and shipyards of Belfast.

Admiral M.D. Naysmith inspected the port and reported:

During my visit to Belfast the lack of AA defence of the port was brought to my notice by all concerned and was particularly keenly felt by the manager of the shipyard who spoke most strongly on the subject.

Apart from the definite requirement from the military aspect I feel that any delay would be a severe test of the loyalty of those splendid Northern Irishmen who are playing such an important part in the national war effort. It is therefore strongly recommended that adequate AA defence, including a balloon barrage, be allocated to Belfast as soon as possible.

Arrangements were immediately put in hand for the anti-aircraft defence of the port of Belfast and the Lough. The requisitioning of the *Ravenswood* formed a small part of those arrangements.

Mr Sydney Robinson recalls seeing her in steam, in the Cumberland Basin on Thursday 11 September, and on the following day in the Royal Edward Dock at Avonmouth, where she took on supplies and coal in readiness for her departure on Sunday 14 September.

On 16 September 1941 she arrived at Belfast, where a survey was commenced by representatives of the Ministry of War Transport – the department established in May 1941 when Winston Churchill combined the Ministries of Transport and Shipping. An entry in the P&A Campbell minute book for 27 October 1941 states, '*Ravenswood* – survey only partially carried out.' It was, however, completed shortly afterwards to the Ministry's satisfaction, and she was then fitted out as an 'Eagle' ship, the Admiralty definition of which was 'A vessel armed and commissioned by the Royal Navy, chiefly for defence against enemy air attack.' The term specifically applied to the hired vessels and came from the first such ships to have been converted for anti-aircraft purposes – the Thames paddle steamers *Royal Eagle* and *Crested Eagle*. On completion of fitting out the *Ravenswood* took up her duties as a harbour guardship in Belfast Lough at the beginning of February 1942.

By that time the Royal Navy's fleet of purpose-built minesweepers had grown considerably and the new vessels gradually superseded the hired paddle steamers. The 7th and 8th Minesweeping Flotillas were disbanded, but there was to be no shortage of work for the paddlers.

In the early summer of 1941 the fury of the Luftwaffe's blitz upon London diminished. The greatest and most prolonged assaults had been on the River Thames and much damage had been inflicted upon the docklands. As far as possible, shipping was being diverted to other ports. This, and the respite in enemy action, afforded the opportunity for some of the damage to be repaired, but the authorities were by no means convinced that the enemy's attempts to destroy the port had ended. In the spring of 1942 ocean traffic began to return to the Thames and plans for additional protection from aerial attack were already being implemented. A part of that additional protection was to be provided by the hired steamers; the six Campbell minesweepers, together with many of their consorts, were converted into Eagle ships.

In mid–February 1942 the *Glen Avon* began refitting at North Shields, and the *Glen Usk* at South Shields. The *Glenmore*, having left the Tyne for the Thames on 15 February, began refitting at Sheerness, and was joined by the *Plinlimmon* and *Westward Ho*, from Granton, in March. The *Skiddaw* also left the Firth of Forth and began refitting at North Shields in mid-May.

By the early summer the *Glen Avon* and *Glen Usk* had been completed and made their way southward to take up their new duties in the lower reaches of the Thames. By June 1942 they had been joined by the *Glenmore*, *Plinlimmon*, *Westward Ho* and *Queen Eagle* as part of the Thames Extended Defence Flotilla, based at Sheerness. The *Skiddaw* was allocated to similar duties but remained, for the time being, on the River Tyne.

Financial Matters

As in the First World War, the records of P&A Campbell contain little information with regard to the hiring charges paid for the steamers; in fact, only three references of any significance appear in the company's minute book.

At the board meeting of Friday 27 October 1939 it was reported that a cheque for £2,628 had been received from the Director of Sea Transport as an advance payment on the hire of the ten requisitioned steamers. Initially the rate of hire of the ships was calculated at 10*s* per gross registered ton, per month, but as in the previous conflict, the rates were the subject of much dispute and negotiation.

On 8 August 1940 the managing director visited the Ministry of Shipping. In an interview with one of the Ministry's representatives, he expressed his dissatisfaction with both the rates of hire and the War Risks Insurance Valuations of the steamers in the event of total loss, and requested that they should be increased. The main points of Mr Banks's submission were:

1. That large sums of money had been spent on the reconditioning of a number of the ships during previous years, particularly the *Britannia*, *Cambria* and *Westward Ho*, thus considerably increasing their value.

2. That the company still incurred heavy organisational expenses by way of the maintenance of its offices in Bristol and the resorts on the Bristol Channel and on the South Coast.

3. That the company had undertaken a large financial commitment by way of the overdraft sanctioned by its bankers for the building of the *Empress Queen*.

4. That the company was still responsible for the running of its engineering shop at the Underfall Yard, Bristol.

The Ministry's representative dealt with the last item first, and stated that as the Underfall Yard was still fully operational and engaged on a programme of engineering work, although not for its own fleet, this could not be taken into consideration and was immediately dismissed. In fact, the war years were exceptionally busy for the Underfall Yard. The company supplied many of the hull fittings for Bristol built frigates, as well as machinery for submarines, and armament production included the supplying of tank and gun parts, torpedo tubes and components for the prefabricated sections of Bailey bridges.

Referring to the other points of Mr Banks's submission, it was stated that the Ministry would be dealing with those matters through the Chamber of Shipping; a course of action which Mr Banks initially found unacceptable. However, it was explained that the Ministry was unable to negotiate with each individual shipowner – its only course was to deal through the Chamber of Shipping with various groups of owners whose ships had been requisitioned and who were similarly situated. This explanation eventually satisfied Mr Banks.

The War Risks Insurance Valuations were later decided upon and were accepted by the company on 5 June 1941 as follows:

Britannia	£22,000
Cambria	£18,000
Westward Ho	£17,000
Glen Avon	£23,000
Glen Usk	£23,500
Glen Gower	£45,000
Waverley	£21,500
Devonia	£24,000
Brighton Queen	£24,000
Brighton Belle	£12,000
Total	£230,000

The inclusion, in the above list, of the three steamers lost at Dunkirk indicates that the question of their compensation had not yet been settled, the Ministry having stated that the amounts of the company's original claims were too high. Negotiations continued until November 1942, and except in the case of the *Devonia*, increased amounts were eventually paid for each of the lost ships.

Interim payments had been made in August 1940 for the *Brighton Queen*, of £19,000; for the *Devonia*, of £18,000; and for the *Brighton Belle*, of £13,000. In August 1941 an interim payment of £21,500 had been made for the *Waverley*. The minutes of the board meeting of Wednesday 25 November 1942 state:

> The secretary reported the receipt of Credit Certificates in respect of the four lost steamers, showing that the sums stated have been placed to the company's credit in the Government Tonnage Replacement Account – Waverley, £5375; Brighton Queen, £6000; Devonia, £6000; Brighton Belle, £3375. Also that letters of Subrogation and Abandonment had been signed.

Mr Banks's tenacity and powers of persuasion had borne fruit; the company received amounts in excess of the valuations of June 1941 of £1,000 for the *Brighton Queen*; £4,375 for the *Brighton Belle*, and £5,375 for the *Waverley*.

Many of the country's seaside piers were 'gapped' during the course of the war. This entailed the removal of sections to prevent their use by sea-borne invaders. In the Bristol Channel, Minehead Pier, owned by P&A Campbell, was not merely gapped but completely demolished on military orders; a fate which was to lead to much legal wrangling in the post-war years regarding compensation. In this view, taken in September 1940, the dismantling of the pier is under way. (Ken Jenkins Collection)

HMS Plinlimmon at the General Steam Navigation Co.'s Yard at Deptford, London, in May 1942. Her conversion from minesweeper to anti-aircraft ship is nearly complete. The Deptford Yard was responsible for maintaining the GSN ships but, during the war, was additionally devoted to naval work; over 300 vessels of all types being dealt with. (Chris Collard Collection)

The White Funnel steamers, now converted to anti-aircraft vessels, at anchor in the lower reaches of the River Thames

HMS Glen Avon, *3 June 1942.* (*From top:* Imperial War Museum. Ref: 1799; Imperial War Museum. Ref: 1800; Imperial War Museum. Ref: 1801.)

HMS Glen Usk, *4 June 1942. (From top:* Imperial War Museum. Ref: 1794; Imperial War Museum. Ref: 1793. *Overleaf* Imperial War Museum. Ref: 1795.)

HMS Glenmore, *5 June 1942.* (*From top:* Imperial War Museum. Ref: 1798; Imperial War Museum. Ref: 1797; Imperial War Museum. Ref: 1796.)

HMS Plinlimmon, *20 October 1942. (From top:* Imperial War Museum. Ref: 1809; Imperial War Museum. Ref: 1810; Imperial War Museum. Ref: 1811.)

HMS Queen Eagle, *1942.* (*Previous page:* Imperial War Museum. Ref: 1790. *This page, from top:* Imperial War Museum. Ref: HU1288; Imperial War Museum. Ref: HU1273; Imperial War Museum. Ref: 1791.)

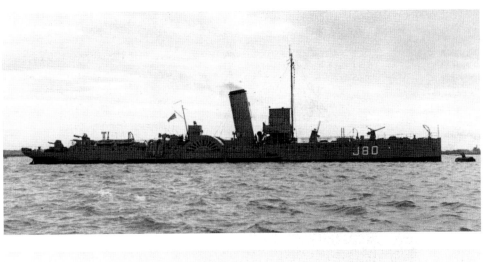

HMS Skiddaw, *1942. (From top:* Imperial War Museum. Ref: HU1257; Imperial War Museum. Ref: HU1249; Imperial War Museum. Ref: HU1258.)

Changing Roles

At night, as officer of the watch, I looked down from the bridge at the guns and their crews standing by at the ready. It seemed a far cry from the days of peace and the holiday crowds. How many, I wondered, would recognise the old Britannia now?

An officer of HMS *Skiddaw*

A period of considerable change and activity for the White Funnel steamers began in the autumn of 1942.

At the end of September the *Glenmore* was relocated at Harwich where she joined the local defence flotilla of anti-aircraft ships. Her place on the Thames was taken by the *Skiddaw*, which was transferred from the Tyne in October.

At the beginning of November the *Glen Avon* and *Glen Usk* sailed from the Thames to Methil, on the Firth of Forth, where they continued to perform their anti-aircraft duties, protecting the assembly points of the east coast convoys in Largo Bay.

HMS Glen Avon *as an anti-aircraft ship in the Firth of Forth during the winter of 1942/1943.* (Imperial War Museum. Ref: 2429)

HMS Glen Usk *as an anti-aircraft ship in the North Sea during the winter of 1942/1943.* (Imperial War Museum. Ref: FL13484)

HMS Glen Usk *as an anti-aircraft ship in the North Sea during the winter of 1942/1943.* (Imperial War Museum. Ref: FL13485)

HMS Glen Avon *as an anti-aircraft ship on the Firth of Forth during the winter of 1942/1943.* (Imperial War Museum. Ref: FL13477)

On 14 November 1942 the *Ravenswood*, still on harbour guard duty at Belfast, was purchased by the Ministry of War Transport. The minutes of the meeting of the Committee for the Purchase of Requisitioned Vessels, of Wednesday 11 November 1942, state:

> *It was agreed that this vessel should be acquired forthwith and settlement offered to the owners [...] subject to adjustment in respect of war damage.*

The offer of £14,500, less an amount of £3,500 recoverable under the War Damage Act owing to the damage caused by the incendiary raid on Bristol in November 1940, was accepted on 19 November 1942. The Ministry's acknowledgement of acceptance to P&A Campbell added: 'In the event of the government deciding to sell the vessel, the Minister is prepared to take all reasonable steps to give you first refusal.'

Mr Keen wrote to Mr Allen:

> *You may say goodbye to the* Ravenswood *and remove her from Campbells' list; she has been bought outright by the Admiralty. I am sorry for I liked the old ship. If the* Empress Queen *comes back I wonder if they will transfer the name to her.* Empress Queen *seems a very poor name.*

The reason for the Admiralty's purchase of the *Ravenswood* is something of a mystery. Of all the Campbell steamers she was the oldest and seemingly most unsuitable for war work – in carrying out her duties as an Eagle ship she had been found unsatisfactory for a variety of reasons.

On 16 October 1942, only eight months after she took up her anti-aircraft duties, her commanding officer, Lt P. O'Driscoll, wrote to the Flag Officer in Charge, Northern Ireland, strongly recommending a reduction in topweight, which was causing problems. He stated:

> While under way the vessel has shown a marked tendency to list with any degree of wind, the lee sponson frequently being underwater and the weather-side paddle hardly immersed. It is thought that the height and weight of the bridge as a whole have contributed to the list to a great extent.

The letter was accompanied by two drawings, reproduced on page 120, showing the bridge as it was and suggested modifications. The alterations, however, were never to be carried out; the situation was to be overtaken by subsequent events.

Lt O'Driscoll's observations brought about a lengthy correspondence with regard to the ship's future. The FOIC(NI) wrote to the Commander-in-Chief, Western Approaches, on 5 November 1942:

> The Ravenswood was commissioned in February 1942 as an Eagle ship for Lough Foyle. As Captain, Londonderry, did not want her she was re-allocated to Belfast for close range defence of vessels anchored in the Lough. She has been of little use as she is only able to protect three or four vessels. Furthermore, an increasing number of ships have anti-aircraft armament comparable to the Ravenswood and do not require the limited extra protection which she can give.
>
> Her low bunker capacity, of about 30 tons, requires her to go to Belfast every three or four days to coal, making her frequently absent from the Lough, and in winter she cannot lie in the exposed anchorage. I suggest re-location to a port where low-flying attack is more probable and where there are valuable craft such as floating docks, ammunition barges, oil lighters etc., requiring protection.

The FOIC(NI) also asked his counterpart in West Wales if she would be of use at Milford Haven but was told that the reasons for her unsuitability at Belfast would apply equally to the Haven.

Other duties were considered for her but the Director of Local Defence at Belfast was reluctant to release her from her anti-aircraft role, despite her inadequacies, because of the possible, more pressing need for Eagle ships during future offensive operations.

On 30 January 1943 the Director of Naval Construction confirmed that as a result of tests recently carried out by his staff, the Ravenswood's seaworthiness was considered satisfactory 'for sheltered waters.' In the light of that information, the Admiralty then proposed that she should join the Local Defence Flotilla based at Sheerness, where, in the calmer waters of the River Thames, her shortcomings would be of lesser consequence.

This suggestion appeared to be the answer, but the passage from Belfast to Sheerness was a cause of anxiety, particularly because of the inadequacy of her pumps. However, the Admiralty stated that suitable pumps could be fitted temporarily, and provided certain other safety measures were complied with, the journey could proceed.

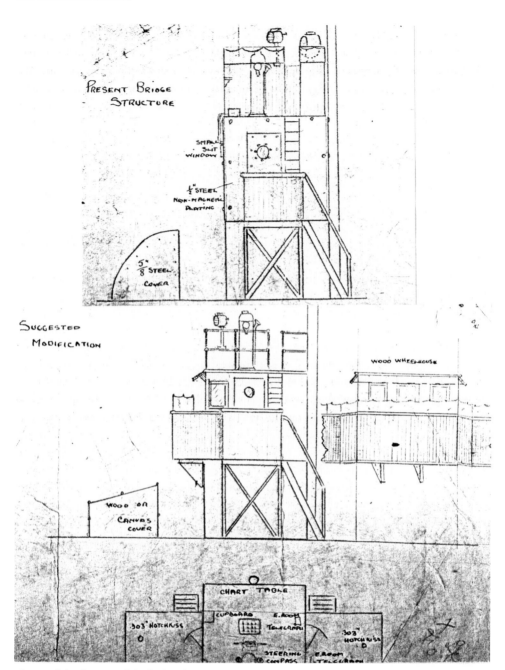

A copy of the drawings of the bridge of HMS Ravenswood, *submitted to the Admiralty by her commander, which accompanied his report detailing the problems of topweight.* (Public Records Office. Ref: ADM1/1623)

Nevertheless, the Director of Local Defence was not convinced. He signalled to the FOIC(NI) that, in his opinion the vessel was unseaworthy and as she was no longer required in Belfast Lough, he suggested that 'she should be moored in the harbour on a C. and M. basis'. (C. and M. being Care and Maintenance, whereby a ship is laid up with a skeleton crew remaining aboard to carry out essential maintenance duties). The FOIC agreed and put the recommendation to the Admiralty; they concurred and the *Ravenswood* was laid up in Belfast from Friday 26 February 1943 – a situation which, however, lasted for only two months.

On 19 April 1943 the FOIC(NI) signalled to the Admiralty:

> *Can a decision be given regarding the* Ravenswood's *future as she is occupying a berth in Belfast which will shortly be required?*

The whole wearisome business began again! This time the Director of Local Defence at Belfast referred the matter to the Director of Sea Transport who suggested her possible use as an accommodation ship. Such a vessel was urgently needed on the Clyde, but the Director of Dockyards summarily dismissed her as being 'quite unsuitable'.

By the end of May the berth which she occupied was urgently required and as a last resort a place was found for her in Liverpool. She was hastily prepared for the voyage across the Irish Sea according to Admiralty instructions, and arrived in the River Mersey at the end of June 1943.

Meanwhile, a plan of a more unusual nature was under consideration for her. In the summer of 1943 the new, four-squadron, Royal Naval Air Station at Burscough, near Ormskirk in Lancashire, was nearing completion. It was the custom of the Royal Naval Air Branch to select a non-seagoing vessel as a 'Nominal Depot Ship'. The chosen vessel had no duties to perform in connection with the air station, but tradition dictated that both should share the same name; consequently it was essential that the vessel should be non-seagoing to avoid confusion. In casting their net in order to find a suitable 'candidate' Air Branch came upon the non-seagoing *Ravenswood*, virtually 'on the doorstep' of the air station. A letter was submitted to the Admiralty stating that it was proposed to name RNAS Burscough, HMS Ringtail. Air Branch explained that a Ringtail was a female hen-harrier, or European Falcon, and added:

> *This appears to be the only British bird of prey whose name has not already been used for some vessel or another, and it is considered ideal for a fighter station.*

It was further proposed that the *Ravenswood*, renamed accordingly, should be the air station's Nominal Depot Ship. If and when she became sea-going again, she would revert to her original name and the air station would then find another, non-seagoing, Nominal Depot Ship. The question was referred to the Ship's Names Committee at the Admiralty, who agreed to the proposal. Thus, from 13 September 1943, two weeks after the commissioning of the air station, HMS *Ravenswood* became HMS *Ringtail*.

Miss Wilcox

You are looking
into this general
question which I
here raise in particular
regard to RINGTAIL.

M Branch II,
Admiralty, S.W. 1.

18th September, 1943.

Dear Dodds,

          With reference to my telephone conversation
with you yesterday and your Reference Sheet A O 1461/43
of 10th September concerning H.M.S. RAVENSWOOD, I have
on second thoughts issued re-naming of the vessel as
H.M.S. RINGTAIL and her commissioning as Nominal Depot
Ship for the R.N. Air Station Burscough as this has, in
fact, taken place.

2.   As I mentioned on the telephone, it is usual
to select a small non-sea-going craft, e.g. a motorboat
or harbour craft, as Nominal Depot Ship as, if a sea-going
vessel is chosen she may be sunk. This would have some
awkward results. H.M.S. RAVENSWOOD (now RINGTAIL) is a
paddler and while she has been reduced to Care and
Maintenance since February 1943 she is always liable to
be re-allocated to a sea-going service, I would therefore suggest that, unless it has been definitely confirmed
that RAVENSWOOD is no longer suitable for sea-going
duties, a small non-sea-going craft should be named H.M.S.
RINGTAIL instead. RAVENSWOOD could then revert to her
original name.

3.   The following papers which I have not seen, all
apparently relate to this matter:- A.O.1461/43,
A.O.1606/43, A.O.D. 78/43.

              Yours sincerely,

G.C.B. Dodds, Esq.,
  Air Branch,
    Dorland House,
      S.W. 1.

*One of the many letters which
circulated in 1943 concerning the
future of HMS* Ravenswood.
(Public Records Office. Ref:
ADM1/13956A)

Life Aboard the *Plinlimmon*

At the end of January 1943, sixteen-year-old Anthony Lambert Hammond completed his
initial Royal Naval training at HMS Raleigh, the shore base at Torpoint, Devon, and joined
his first ship, HMS *Plinlimmon*. In conversation with the author, 'Wally' Hammond
(nicknamed after the famous Gloucestershire and England cricketer of the time) recalled the
early months of his distinguished naval career aboard the Campbell paddler:

> *I joined the Sheerness Naval Base, HMS Wildfire, and was drafted to the* Plinlimmon. *She
> was manned by a Devonport crew as part of the Thames Extended Defence Flotilla; the
> Flotilla Commander at that time being Captain Cordeaux RN Retd. The other ships of the
> flotilla were the Clyde paddler,* Jeanie Deans; *the south coast paddler,* Lorna Doone; *the
> Thames paddlers,* Golden Eagle *and* Royal Eagle; *the Campbell turbine steamer,* Queen
> Eagle; *and the screw steamer,* Douwe Aukes, *a former Royal Netherlands Navy minelayer
> of 748gt dating from 1922.*
>
> > *We moored at buoys in Sheerness but spent most of our time on convoy escort duties between
> > Harwich and the North Foreland. Most of the vessels which we escorted were colliers, carrying coal
> > from the north to the London power stations. At night we often anchored in the Thames estuary,
> > near the forts, where we plotted the fall of magnetic mines from the German minelaying aircraft.*

Sixteen-year-old Anthony Lambert Hammond, on 30 January 1943. Having completed his initial training at HMS Raleigh, Devonport, he was about to join his first ship, HMS Plinlimmon. *(By courtesy of Lt-Com. A.L. Hammond)*

There were many wrecks in the estuary, mainly from ships striking the magnetic mines, and the river was full of all sorts of debris which resulted in a good deal of paddle trouble. That was one of the reasons why the paddlers were such popular ships in which to serve – they spent so much time in dock under repair!

They made ideal anti-aircraft ships – plenty of deck space. Our armament included five machine-guns, one of which was mounted in a Boulton and Paul, perspex covered turret – mainly intended for aircraft. My own action station was at the rocket launcher at the stern. This was a most unpopular piece of equipment; we only used it once and several of us were burned! We were not really involved in the air defence of the harbour and only met enemy aircraft on a few occasions when a Junkers or Heinkel fired on us – and missed.

We coaled frequently from the coal hulk. This was a very hard and filthy job which necessitated a good washing down of both the ship and ourselves afterwards. There was not the luxury of hot water and our 'baths' consisted of pouring a bucket of cold water over us. It was always a good idea to 'keep in' with the stokers who would often take our buckets of water to the boiler room to heat them up.

The accommodation was not at all bad, I never had to sling a hammock in the Plinlimmon, *there were bunks for all of us. The food, too, was good; in fact, we probably ate better than the civilian population. It seems incredible now but the Admiralty allowed an amount of 1/1d per day to feed each rating. How much food could you buy these days for the equivalent 5p?!*

We were on canteen messing, the system whereby a leading seaman would be put in charge of the provisions for a mess of ten men. He would decide on the menu and prepare the food for cooking, and was therefore excused from the mundane deck duties such as chipping, painting and so on. After preparing the food he would take it, on trays, to the galley to be cooked, a brass tally with the mess number having been attached to each tray. The next time he would see it would be when 'cooks to the galley' was piped and he collected the cooked dishes.

We had our daily rum ration of course – four measures of rum to equal measures of water for ratings; neat for the officers.

Our tobacco was supplied duty free and cost us 2/4d per pound for either leaf, for the pipe smokers, or 'Tickler' tobacco for cigarettes – so called because the tins resembled those which contained Tickler's Jam.

It was fascinating to watch the older sailors making up their 'pricks' (correctly 'periques') of tobacco. The leaves were laid out flat and layered with their rum rations. The leaves were then rolled up, wrapped in a piece of cloth and parcelled up in spunyarn impregnated with tar. This was left for some time to mature, and when ready for use the spunyarn and cloth were removed. The solid stick of tobacco was then cut into slices and rubbed between the hands for smoking. The sale of the tobacco to our dockyard 'mateys' was a lucrative business – all highly illegal of course, but common practice among the older 3-badgers or 'stripeys' – the men who had been awarded 3 good conduct badges or stripes. A good conduct badge was awarded for every four years of good behaviour, or as the sailors themselves put it – four years of 'undetected crime'.

Wally enjoyed his time in the *Plinlimmon*, and it represented a solid foundation for his naval career. After only a few months he was sent to HMS Alfred, in Brighton, to begin officer training and he eventually retired having attained the rank of Lieutenant Commander.

Accommodation Ships

Early in 1943 the Admiralty proposed that many of the hired paddle steamers should be paid off and returned to their owners, but before de-commissioning consideration was given to other duties for which they might be suitable.

The *Plinlimmon* was transferred from the Thames to Harwich in mid-May as a replacement for the *Glenmore* which was then paid off and laid up. Plans, however, changed frequently and in June 1943 the *Glenmore* was called up again and sent to Rochester, on the River Medway, to be converted into an accommodation ship.

At about the same time the *Plinlimmon* developed boiler trouble and an inspection revealed that her 'haystack' boiler was no longer operational; she was, accordingly, paid off in mid-July. It appears that P&A Campbell were then expected to bear the cost of her towage from Harwich to Bristol – a course of action which the company found unacceptable. An entry in the minute book for 20 July 1943 states:

> Re. Plinlimmon. *A letter was received from the Ministry of War Transport on 12 July 1943 with regard to the release of this vessel from naval service. After discussion the secretary was instructed to reply – "my directors point out that what appears to them to be your greatest difficulty is the removal of the vessel from the Thames Estuary. They are of the opinion that the Admiralty themselves can despatch the vessel to any port which would be most convenient, particularly as you say that there is a likelihood of her services being required at some future date. Also, they are unaware of any clause in the T98 charter whereby a ship could be returned under the arrangements you suggest.*

The matter, however, was not pursued as, almost immediately, the Ministry of War Transport informed P&A Campbell that alternative work had been secured for her in London. She was towed from Harwich to the Thames in late July 1943 and began fitting out as an accommodation ship.

The Flag Officer in Charge at Harwich now found himself short of an anti-aircraft ship and requested a replacement. The *Glenmore's* conversion for accommodation purposes had not yet started so she was chosen to return to Harwich where, once again, she became part of the flotilla of anti-aircraft ships, escorting the east coast convoys from the Essex port into the Thames estuary.

The *Queen Eagle* was released from her anti-aircraft duties and paid off in September 1943. She reverted to her original name of *Empress Queen* and was taken in hand at a Tilbury shipyard where extensive alterations were made to her accommodation. The Ministry of War Transport then placed her under the management of the General Steam Navigation Co. of London and on 7 January 1944 she commenced running between Stranraer and Larne as a services personnel transport, becoming known to many as the 'Leave Ship'. She ran on this service in conjunction with the GSN's own screw vessel, *Royal Daffodil*.

125

Above and below: *The* Empress Queen *as a troop transport in 1944. The location is unknown but is probably either Stranraer or Larne.* (H.G. Owen Collection)

Throughout 1943 the preparations for the forthcoming invasion of occupied France were gaining momentum, and an increasing number of personnel were converging on southern England. In the West Country the naval sub-station at Dartmouth was becoming seriously overcrowded. It was the base for, among other vessels, the 15th Motor Gunboat Flotilla, part of the growing coastal defence force. Four additional such vessels had been purchased from Turkey and with the influx of their crews and extra maintenance personnel, HMS Dartmouth was reaching saturation point. Accommodation ships, moored in the River Dart, appeared to be the ideal solution to the problem.

In March 1943 the *Westward Ho* and Cosens' South Coast paddler, *Emperor of India*, were due to be paid off in London. Dartmouth's Director of Local Defence inspected the two ships and considered them to be suitable for accommodation purposes. He wrote to the Admiralty:

> *It would be the intention to moor these two ships alongside each other in the River Dart, for administration as a single unit, and for the motor gunboats to lie outside their paddle boxes. The present anti-aircraft armament of the paddle steamers would not be required beyond two Oerlikons for each ship.*

It was later decided that the requirements for accommodation could be met with just one ship and that the slightly larger of the two, the *Westward Ho*, would be the more suitable. In June 1943 she was withdrawn from her anti-aircraft duties on the Thames and was sent to Rochester where she was fitted out for her new role, which included the construction of a number of most unsightly steel 'sheds' on her promenade deck. She had been completed by the autumn and then made her way to Chatham for further maintenance. It was not until 3 December 1943 that she left the dockyard, in tow, with a care and maintenance party aboard, bound for South Devon. After many delays owing to bad weather, she was moored to buoys in the River Dart and commissioned on 1 January 1944 as a tender to HMS Dartmouth, to act not only as an accommodation ship but also as a store ship and workshop.

In addition to their coastal defensive role the motor gunboats were involved in transporting agents to and from the French coast. Furthermore, the high-speed vessels were frequently the last link in a chain of highly successful escape operations, organised by the French Resistance, to repatriate RAF and US airmen who had been forced to bail out of their aircraft over France. These dangerous night manoeuvres were usually preceded by briefings from their commanding officers in the wardroom of the *Westward Ho*. She was instrumental in many such clandestine activities and to this end had been installed with direct telephone communications with the Commander of Local Operations at his office in the Dartmouth Naval College, the Commander in Chief at Plymouth and the Deputy Director of Defence at the Admiralty.

Several months after her arrival at Dartmouth a most curious proposal was put forward. In May 1944 the Ministry of War Transport informed P&A Campbell that the *Westward Ho's* boiler had been condemned and that the Ministry would meet the cost of its replacement. This was a very strange decision; the ships chosen for accommodation puposes were invariably those which had reached the end of their careers and were most unlikely to sail again. However, Barclay & Curle of Glasgow were asked to undertake the work, but the reboiling never, in fact, took place. The reason for the change of plan is unconfirmed but must surely

HMS Westward Ho *as an accommodation ship in the River Dart, 1944.* (Chris Collard Collection)

have been that the Ministry considered the reboiling of a fifty-year-old, non-operational paddle steamer in deteriorating condition to be false economy.

Accommodation ships were also required at a number of other ports on the South Coast, specifically for the personnel responsible for the maintenance of the ships destined to take part in the invasion of France. The Flag Officer in Charge at London was asked by the Admiralty if he had any vessels available for this purpose. On 24 February 1944 he replied that the *Plinlimmon* was laid up in the Eastern Docks, in company with the Clyde paddler, *Queen Empress*, and the South Coast paddler, *Princess Elizabeth*. A care and maintenance party consisting of two officers, an engineer officer, and twenty-four ratings were looking after the three ships. He stated that the *Queen Empress* and *Princess Elizabeth* would be available to sail at seventy-two hours notice, but the Admiralty had issued orders that the *Plinlimmon* was not to be steamed owing to the condition of her boiler.

The Admiralty did not consider using either the *Queen Empress* or *Princess Elizabeth* and were unwilling to extend their hire. The *Plinlimmon* would have been suitable, and could have been towed to the south coast, but as the two former vessels were shortly to be paid off the *Plinlimmon*'s services were still required in London. Consequently, the Admiralty searched farther afield for an alternative vessel.

During the course of their search HMS *Ringtail* came to their attention. While the Admiralty appreciated the fact that her small size would provide only limited accommodation; that she had not been in steam for nearly six months, and that her seaworthiness had previously been called into question, a report on her condition was requested from the Flag Officer in Charge at Liverpool. His brief reply stated:

HMS Ringtail

Speed	*12 knots.*
Endurance	*36 hours continuous steaming.*
Hull	*Reasonably good.*
Stability	*Poor.*
Engines	*Reasonably good.*
	Ready in four days.

An Admiralty letter to the FOIC Liverpool, dated 17 March 1944, confirmed that HMS *Ringtail* would revert to her original name of *Ravenswood* and, despite her limitations, would be used instead of the *Plinlimmon* as an accommodation ship, on the South Coast.

Her arrival on the South Coast in April 1944 coincided with that of HMS *Ambassador* (Cosens' paddle steamer, *Embassy*) from the River Tyne. Both vessels were placed under the Plymouth Special Service Command and were based in Torquay harbour. Although originally intended for use as accommodation ships, and designated as such in the Red List, other duties took priority. They were kept particularly busy ferrying personnel and supplies to and from the harbours which served the South Devon and Cornish camps, as well as acting as tenders to the ever growing armada of vessels assembling and preparing for the imminent offensive on the shores of occupied France.

INVASION

Conditions were bad [...] but the weather experts gave some promise of a temporary improvement on the morning of the 6th. After this, they predicted a return of rough weather for an indefinite period [...] General Eisenhower [...] chose to go ahead with the operation [...] the die was irrevocably cast; the invasion would be launched on 6th June.

Years of meticulous planning for the Allied invasion of France came to fruition on Tuesday 6 June 1944, when British, American and Canadian troops landed on the coast of Normandy. 'Overlord' was an operation of monumental proportions, made all the more difficult by the need for the extensive training and preparation to be hidden from German eyes. Many diversionary tactics were instituted and the Allied strategists kept the enemy guessing as to where the actual landings would take place. Even when they received news of the landings, the German High Command remained convinced that Normandy was another diversion, and that the main invasion would be at Calais.

Of the eight remaining steamers of the White Funnel fleet, the *Glen Avon* and *Skiddaw* played a direct part in 'Operation Overlord'; the *Glen Usk*, *Glenmore*, *Ravenswood* and *Westward Ho* were involved indirectly, while the *Plinlimmon* remained in London acting as an accommodation ship, and the *Empress Queen* continued her troop carrying duties between Scotland and Northern Ireland.

The *Skiddaw* was the last of the White Funnel steamers to leave the Thames flotilla, and on 28 May 1944 she arrived off Dungeness where she anchored in company with many other vessels detailed to guard a number of the concrete piers of the 'Mulberry' harbour. Beginning on D-Day, these 60ft high 'blocks of flats', as the service men called them, were towed across the English Channel to the Normandy coast. It was a long, slow process made all the more harrowing by the constant threat of enemy attack. They were accompanied on their journey by flotillas of anti-aircraft ships, and the *Skiddaw* was one of them.

On 14 June she was transferred to Portsmouth Command and ordered to take her place at an anchorage at Peel Bank, off the coast of the Isle of Wight between Cowes and Fishbourne. There, her duties as an 'HQ ship' included a multitude of tasks; her main activities involving her in the sea training of Army and Air Force personnel.

She was also used to provide food for the many troops making their way to the 'Far shore', as the Normandy coast was called at the time. It was estimated that she served 14,500 hot meals within about two weeks; an incredible achievement when one considers that the galley was designed to cater for a proportion of her normal peacetime complement of under 1,000 passengers and crew.

Great credit must also be afforded to the catering personnel who, under what must have been very difficult conditions, accounted for the troops' consumption of eight tons of potatoes, 1,100 tins of dried milk, 2,300lbs of bread, 2,000lbs of meat, 625lbs of sugar and

Right and below: *HMS
Skiddaw at her anchorage off
the Isle of Wight in 1944.*
(Ken Jenkins Collection)

575lbs of cabbages. However, the increasing demands put upon her in this direction, led to her replacement by the New Medway Steam Packet Co.'s paddler, *Queen of Thanet*, whose catering facilities were apparently more suited to the task. The latter was due to have been paid off but was retained and re-located at the Peel Bank anchorage, while the *Skiddaw* returned to her anti-aircraft duties in the Thames estuary at the beginning of July.

The Nore War Diary records:

> 25/26 July 1944
> *HMS* Skiddaw *destroyed one flying bomb by gunfire in the estuary.* HMS Jeanie Deans *also claims one shot down.*

The *Glenmore* was detached from her convoy escort duties at Harwich at the beginning of July, and after some weeks under repair at Lowestoft, was reported as having arrived at Portsmouth on 6 August. This visit, however, was very brief. She proceeded to Chatham for further repairs and maintenance which were completed by 1 September, before resuming anti-aircraft duties on the Thames.

The Nore War Diary states:

> 8/9 November 1944
> *HMS* Glenmore *and HMS* Skiddaw *each shot down one flying bomb while moored alongside each other.*

The officers and crew of HMS Skiddaw. *Neither the date nor the location is known.* (Peter Southcombe Collection)

On the South Coast, following D–Day, the duties of the *Ravenswood* and *Ambassador* gradually diminished and consideration was given to their future, which included a somewhat curious plan. The Plymouth War Diary includes the following report from the Naval Officer in Charge, Torquay:

15 August 1944.
Lt W.C. Gilbert RNVR, Port Amenities Liaison Officer, Dartmouth, called to inspect Ravenswood *and* Ambassador *regarding the possibility of fitting one out as a showboat.*

Exactly what kind of 'showboat' was not detailed but both ships escaped the potentially undignified fate. The *Ambassador* was decommissioned at the end of the year and eventually returned to her owners in September 1945. The *Ravenswood*, still the property of the Royal Navy, sailed from Torquay, on Sunday 20 August 1944, to Plymouth, where she was laid up in the River Tamar, off Devonport, and held in reserve pending further duties.

Meanwhile, the *Glen Usk* and *Glen Avon* had left the Firth of Forth and sailed south to Spithead in response to an Admiralty order, dated 14 July, to the Commander in Chief, Rosyth, which stated:

Glen Usk *and* Glen Avon *urgently required by Portsmouth Command. [...] Request vessels may be sailed to Portsmouth as soon as possible.*

The two ships formed part of the force anchored in St Helen's Roads, off the north-east coast of the Isle of Wight, specifically detailed to guard against the enemy's latest weapon, the long range rockets which were being unleashed in large numbers on southern England from their bases on the French coast.

A Tragic Loss

After two weeks off the Isle of Wight the *Glen Avon* was transferred to the Normandy coast, where she fulfilled a dual role as an examination vessel and guard ship, off Port-en-Bessin, in Seine Bay. It was on this station that she met her end under most unfortunate circumstances. The report of her loss, submitted to the Admiralty by her commanding officer, Lt E.V. Symons RNVR (temporarily acting as Lieutenant Commander), gives a graphic account of the terri-fying events of her last few hours:

To the Naval Officer in Charge, Arromanches,
I have the honour to report that HMS Glen Avon *was lost at sea through stress of weather at approximately midnight on Saturday 2 September 1944, in Seine Bay.*
Position 340 degrees, Ver Sur Mer light – 2 miles.
    There had been a strong wind all day, veering from the southward to WNW and increasing in force until, at 21.00, it was force 8 and more in the gusts, which veered to the north-west, increasing sea and swell. At first my chief concern was for the port sponson, which was known to be weak, and permission was granted for the ship to enter the western anchorage. This proved

impossible as the anchors could not be heaved in, nor the cable slipped. The ship had been dragging for some time and the engines had been put at dead slow ahead to slow ahead to prevent too much drift.

At about 21.30 it was reported to me that there were three inches of water in the forward magazine; this is situated below the seamen's mess deck and is reached by a hatch and companionway. The anchor-chain locker is reached by going through a steel door in the bulkhead which separates it from the magazine. The water was obviously coming from the hawse pipes, flooding the capstan flat on the main deck, and pouring down the navel pipe into the seamen's mess deck. It should be explained that the hawse pipes are fitted only 18 inches to two feet above the water line of the ship in her present trim as an Eagle ship, her equipment having increased her peace-time draught. It was not unusual to have water in the magazine in bad weather, but hitherto the ship's pumps have coped with the situation. This time, however, the portable petrol engine could not be started. As the depth of the water was increasing the ship went down by the head until the hawse pipes were under the water line. They had already been plugged with hammocks and shoring, but the water still came in. All hands had been employed baling with buckets, but in a short time it was reported that there were five feet of water in the magazine. I made a request for tugs and went down to inspect the magazine. When I arrived it was filled almost to the deckhead and the situation was obviously desperate. It was still impossible to free the anchors and I attempted to part the cable by going ahead and astern, but I could not turn the ship, although it was noticed that she responded best by going astern, the wind blowing her inshore. It was then my intention to beach her, as I considered that she would sink before the tugs could get her to Arromanches.

I regret that from then on I lost track of time, and my First Lieutenant, who might have assisted me in this report, is unfortunately among those missing. Rockets were fired and signal lanterns shone to guide craft coming in to assist us. The lower deck was cleared and fallen in aft, and the forward fresh water tanks were pumped empty. Normally there is between two and three feet freeboard to the sponsons, from where the sea would have access to the main deck via the four sponson doors and two doors leading to the paddles. The ship heeled over to the wind, the forward port sponson doors burst open and water rushed in along the engine room alleyway on the main deck. By this time, approximately 23.00, the tug, Storm King, was alongside, with motor minesweeper No 266 in attendance. I asked Storm King if she could beach us, but she was handicapped by her 18ft draught. She succeeded in coming alongside on our port quarter in an attempt to take off the ship's company, who were standing by to abandon ship. Two succeeded in jumping aboard the tug, but the position was much too dangerous for her to remain, and I think she damaged her bows. Our quarter was certainly stove in as the ships heeled in the heavy swell. I then gave the order to abandon ship, and the tug and motor minesweeper stood off to pick up my men who got away on carley floats where possible. By this time Glen Avon had heeled 45° to port and as the bridge was untenable (it collapsed soon afterwards) I directed operations from the rails on the starboard side amidships, the ship then lying with her port side completely submerged. Eventually the Engineer Officer, about seven ratings and myself were left on board. These men had not responded to my order to abandon ship, and two of them had been hauled back on board previously in response to their cries for help.

The end must have come at 23.52, as I later found that my watch had stopped at that time. The ship sank beneath us. I wish to record my appreciation of the magnificent efforts of motor *minesweeper No 266 which rescued 45 officers and men, and the tug which picked up 22 officers and men in the most difficult conditions, and for the hospitality and treatment received on board those ships.*

Of the eight officers, including myself, and 77 ratings on board, one officer and twelve ratings are missing. Two ratings died after being picked up. The spirit on board was very good right up to the end and everyone did his best to save the ship. I wish to record the good services in this direction of the First Lieutenant, Sub. Lt J.P.C. Wilkinson RNVR; Chief Engineer, Lt (E) Alec Campbell RNR; Sub Lt B.M. Clegg RNVR; Sub Lt P.E. Nicholls RNVR; Chief Engineman W.C. Gullam; Petty Officer Stephens; Leading Seaman F.H. Battshill and Leading Seaman J.F. Stokes.

The commanding officer of motor minesweeper No.266, Lt D.J. Else, also submitted a report to the Admiralty, in which he stated that on the night in question his vessel was at anchor, riding out the force 8 gale. At 23.15 he sighted the *Glen Avon's* distress rockets in a south-easterly direction, and proceeded immediately, with the tug *Storm King*, to give assistance. By the time he reached her she was breaking up and the crew had taken to the water. By about 02.15 on Sunday 3 September he had taken aboard forty-six survivors, one of whom was transferred to HMS *Ambitious* for medical attention. No other survivors were seen and he then had to abandon the search as his ship was being blown close inshore.

The loss of the *Glen Avon* claimed the lives of fifteen of the men who served in her, several of whom were buried in the Ryes Military Cemetery, near Bazenville.

It was a tragedy brought about by a most unfortunate series of circumstances: the increased draught of the vessel, the close proximity of the hawse pipes to sea level, her pitching in the heavy seas, the fouling of both anchors, the influx of water, and finally the failure of her pumps. Each one of these circumstances in itself may not have proved fatal, but their combined effect culminated in the flooding of the chain locker making access impossible for the freeing of the anchor chains from the bulkhead to which they were shackled.

Immediately following the tragedy, questions were asked within the Admiralty. A copy of the Seaworthiness Instructions, issued by the Director of Naval Construction's department, was produced. These instructions had been sent to the Commander in Chief of The Nore in May 1942, when the *Glen Avon* first became an Eagle ship in the Thames estuary, and stated:

Investigation of the inclining experiment results has been made. It is requested that the following instructions be issued to the commanding officer – Your ship has been inclined and her seaworthiness is considered satisfactory for her present service as an Eagle ship in sheltered waters, provided the maximum coal carried does not exceed 35 tons. Any unnecessary items or stores not required for her present service should be landed at the first opportunity.

To begin with, Portsmouth Command was asked to explain why, in the light of the above report, the *Glen Avon* was sent to the French coast in the first instance. The Admiralty's letter included the following paragraph:

The Glen Avon was transferred from Rosyth to Portsmouth Command for employment in the sheltered waters of Spithead. [...] The Director of Local Defence is not aware of the authority on which the vessel was transferred to the far shore, and it is unfortunate that a vessel suitable only for 'sheltered waters' should have been exposed to the open sea in bad weather conditions.

The Commander in Chief at Portsmouth replied that on the morning of 18 August he received an urgent request from the Flag Officer of the British Activity Area in Normandy for a replacement for a vessel which had been torpedoed; the only available vessel was the *Glen Avon*. Before she sailed from Portsmouth it was confirmed by the staff of the Naval Officer in Charge at Arromanches that she would be acceptable, even though only a small paddle steamer.

The Director of Defence then added his comments and began by confirming that the Commander in Chief, Portsmouth, was required by the Flag Officer in Normandy to meet an urgent operational need, and used the only available vessel. He continued:

> *It is not clear whether any special warning had been given to the C-in-C about the unseaworthy qualities of the* Glen Avon. *[...] While it was certainly known at Portsmouth, when they sailed her, that she was only a small paddle ship it was also known that she had made the passage from Rosyth just previously, and that she had been in the Firth of Forth before that.*
>
> *It was also considered that it was a reasonable conclusion that she was fit to operate off the French coast, in August, in the lee of a Mulberry harbour for shelter. The NOIC at Arromanches was, in any case, content to accept the* Glen Avon *without raising the question of her seaworthiness.*
>
> *It is therefore concluded that the loss must be regarded as one of the hazards of war accentuated by exceptional stress of weather for this time of year. [...]*

This appeared to satisfy the Admiralty as to why the *Glen Avon* was sent to the Normandy coast.

The circumstances of her loss were clear from Lt-Com. Symons's report but the Director of Defence added to the above summary:

> *To guard against any repetition of this loss it may be considered worthwhile for the Admiralty to draw attention to the importance of realising that the ground tackle and cable working arrangements of most merchant vessels is not up to Naval standards. In the case of the* Glen Avon *the anchors would not hold and the cables could not be slipped. If they could have been slipped it is probable that she could have saved herself. It is likely that these deficiencies could be improved in small ways when the Navy takes over a merchant vessel for service.*

The Director of Local Defence then became involved and commented:

> *It would appear from the difficulties encountered in endeavouring to slip the cables that this vessel was not equipped with Blake stoppers, as would be the case in a naval vessel.*
>
> *In view of the large number of small vessels requisitioned for war service it would not be practical, for considerations of time, labour and material, to fit all these vessels with Blake stoppers, and in these circumstances the peace-time arrangements of the anchors and cables have to be accepted. [...]*

Provided it had been realised in time that it might be necessary to slip the cables, they could have been stoppered on deck with wire stoppers, thus leaving enough slack in the locker to get the pins out of the shackles. The Blake stopper is useful but not essential. It is suggested that the Director of Navigation might draft a short Admiralty Fleet Order to highlight the problem.

The Director of Navigation, however, was not at all disposed to do so. He wrote:

The real reason for these unforeseen incidents is lack of seamanship and it is not considered that this would be remedied by an Admiralty Fleet Order. No further action is therefore proposed.

The Director of Local Defence replied:

The real reason may, as the Director of Navigation states, be lack of seamanship but I cannot see that it is an argument for not issuing a warning. However, I do not wish to press the point.

The matter was finally brought to a close by the Flag Officer, British Activity Area, Normandy, who signalled to the Admiralty:

It is not intended to convene a Board of Inquiry to investigate this loss, since it is considered that the facts are clear and that no useful purpose would be served thereby.

The gale on the night of 2/3 September, which reached force 9 at times, caused distress to other ships in the vicinity, which accounts for tugs not being available to provide assistance earlier or in greater numbers. [...]

Taking all circumstances into consideration I am of the opinion that Acting Temporary Lieutenant Commander E. T. Symons RNVR took all possible action to save his ship and no blame is attributable to him for the loss.

The *Glen Avon* came to rest on the seabed a couple of miles off the coast and became partially exposed as the tide receded. A correspondent of the writer, Mr Derek W. Spiers, was an Army officer in charge of a beach group on the night she foundered. He states: 'I was surprised to see only the mast and funnel of the *Glen Avon* on the morning of 3 September off Courseulles.'

Another correspondent, Mr Bill Shields, joined the *Glen Avon* at Wallsend-on-Tyne in May 1942 as an AA3 Gunner, and remained with her until her loss. In recalling her personnel he particularly remembers her Chief Engineer, Alec Campbell (one of the two sons of Capt. Peter Campbell). Alec was very much a 'father figure' aboard the ship. He was a jovial character with a very optimistic outlook on life who, however, was always exhorting the crew to 'go easy on the water'. The *Glen Avon*'s freshwater tanks held a limited supply and their replenishment was not always easy.

Mr Shields recalls that although the gale of 2 September was particularly severe, the ship was refused permission to enter the confines of the Mulberry harbour, owing to the potential danger to the ships already inside, until late in the evening. By that time the anchor chain locker was filling rapidly and he vividly remembers being one of the party detailed to plug the hawse pipes with hammocks to stem the influx of water.

The order to abandon ship was particularly worrying for him as he was a non-swimmer. One of his shipmates stood alongside him on the after deck and advised him to wait until a big sea came along and then to jump overboard. This he did, and supported by his lifejacket, made his way to a crowded carley float to which he clung until being picked up and taken ashore by the motor minesweeper 266.

On the following morning he made his way to the beach and saw the wreck of the ship which had been his home for over two years, resting on the seabed.

Two months later P&A Campbell were informed by the Ministry of War Transport that consideration was being given to the salving of the *Glen Avon*. However, nothing more was heard of the matter until the end of February 1945 when the Ministry was advised by the Admiralty that 'as the vessel broke up in a recent gale' such an attempt would be pointless.

It has often been asserted that the *Glen Avon* was accompanied to the Normandy coast by the *Glen Usk* and that the two ships were similarly employed. This was not, in fact, the case. The Admiralty records show that the *Glen Usk* remained in the vicinity of the Isle of Wight, under Portsmouth Command, until being paid off in November 1944. She was then placed in the hands of the Director of Sea Transport and held in reserve in Portsmouth harbour, pending further duties.

Antwerp

Following the D-Day landings the Allied troops continued their thrust through France and Belgium towards Germany, but as their bases in Normandy were left farther behind, the problem of supplies became acute. With the capture of Antwerp by the Allies on 2 September 1944, arrangements were set in motion to clear a channel from the southern North Sea to the entrance of the Scheldt and upriver to its harbour.

On the evening of 4 November 1944 the first minesweepers reached Antwerp after one of the largest and most intricate sweeping operations of the war. The first three coasters reached the port on 26 November, and on the same day it was reported that 219 berths had been made available to allied shipping. Ammunition, food, fuel and transport could now be supplied to within sixty miles of the troops. A convoy of eighteen ships, including HMS *Skiddaw*, reached Antwerp safely on 28 November, and on 1 December over 10,000 tons of stores were landed.

The *Glenmore* arrived at Antwerp on 4 December; both she and the *Skiddaw* having been allocated to the Allied Naval Command, X Force, as part of the Eagle Flotilla.

The *Glenmore* was now under the command of Lt-Com. Lachlan Shedden. He had been her Chief Officer in the years preceding the war and her First Lieutenant following her requisition, before being promoted as a result of his outstanding service, particularly at Dunkirk. He remained with her for the duration of the war.

Flying bombs and rockets plagued Antwerp and its harbour for some time and both White Funnel steamers fell victim to sporadic enemy attack; the *Glenmore* receiving a most unwelcome 'Christmas present' on 24 December 1944. Lt-Com. Shedden's report to the Naval Officer in Charge states:

A German long-range rocket projectile fell into the water, bearing approximately 155 degrees on the port side, at an estimated range of 40 to 50 yards. It is thought probable that the rocket struck the river bed before exploding as a quantity of black mud was thrown over the ship, and a few fragments which were collected on board after the occurrence were more than two feet in length. One such fragment which fell on the port sponson was coated in ice to a thickness of half an inch.

The damage by the blast far exceeded that caused by fragments; all canvas wind dodgers around the guns were torn adrift, portholes on the port quarter were splintered, water tanks below decks were expanded, the forward companionway collapsed and the Commanding Officer's upper deck cabin was wrecked.

Shrapnel which entered the ship's side in four places appeared to come at a horizontal, about eight feet from the waterline, piercing steel plate of $\frac{3}{16}$ inch, and woodwork of approximately $\frac{3}{4}$ inch. Other pieces embedded themselves in the woodwork of the bridge – one inflicting a thigh wound on the officer of the watch after passing through the $\frac{1}{2}$-inch wooden door to the bridge, 27 feet above deck level.

Damage below decks was not considerable – articles were thrown on the deck from the racks and shelves; screws supporting air conduits and woodwork enclosing electrical leads were torn adrift; the bath was lifted sideways and about a foot from its normal position, also washbasins collapsed. The outer covering of the port paddle box was stove in.

As far as can be ascertained, at the time of this report, no damage was sustained by the engine room and no structural damage is apparent to the machinery (in course of examination).

Casualties – four slightly wounded, two with severe shock, and several other ratings with superficial injuries treated on board.

Although repairs were carried out, this incident effectively marked the end of the *Glenmore's* naval service. The Red List entry for 31 December 1944 states, '*Glenmore* to be paid off.'

She did, however, remain in Belgian waters for a further six months, during which time, under the management of the General Steam Navigation Co. Ltd of London, she was employed as a transport for RAF personnel in connection with the Scheldt Balloon Barrage.

The *Skiddaw* also remained in the Scheldt and continued her anti-aircraft duties. On 1 January 1945, during one of the last enemy raids on Antwerp before the liberation of Belgium and Holland, she was hit by a shell which penetrated the wireless cabin, damaged the equipment, and wounded the operator. He was taken to the sick bay while Leading Telegraphist Geoffrey Fisher, with the help of an assistant, repaired the apparatus while still under fire. For his gallant action, Geoffrey Fisher was subsequently awarded the Distinguished Service Medal. The citation states:

Despite severe shock and the wireless cabin being a shambles, he proceeded to carry out his duties and he personally put up a new aerial to transmit urgent operational signals without delay. He refused medical attention until all danger had passed.

The *Skiddaw's* Commanding Officer, Lt A.D. Hewett RNVR, and Chief Engineer, Lt (E) Hector McFadyen RNVR, were mentioned in Despatches.

She narrowly escaped further damage, this time from a V2 rocket, on 28 January 1945 while lying alongside a riverside berth in Antwerp. On this occasion it was her flotilla consort, the New Medway Steam Packet Co.'s paddle steamer, *Queen of Kent*, moored ahead of her, which was on the receiving end; the rocket exploding only a few yards from her hull. The crew of the *Skiddaw* rendered every assistance, but tragically ten of the *Queen of Kent's* ratings were killed and fifteen were injured. Despite extensive damage the vessel was repaired in Antwerp and returned to her anti-aircraft duties about a month later.

On 5 April 1945 the Flag Officer in Charge at Belgium wrote to the Allied Naval Command, X Force:

> *Six Eagle ships are based at Antwerp – four being normally operational for use on the Scheldt. Their upkeep requires a large amount of repair work which might be better devoted to other ships. In view of the very much reduced air threat and high cost of manpower and maintenance these ships could now be dispensed with and returned to the UK.*

The six ships referred to were HMS *Aristocrat* (the Clyde paddle steamer *Talisman*); HMS *Scawfell* (the Clyde paddler *Jupiter*); HMS *Goatfell* (the Clyde paddler *Caledonia*); HMS *Royal Eagle*; HMS *Queen of Kent* and HMS *Skiddaw*.

Several alternative duties were then considered for the *Skiddaw*, one being to release her to the Director of Sea Transport, 'to meet a 'Red Ensign' requirement in the Solent', and another to provide accommodation for the Senior Naval Officer of Operation 'Pluto' (Pipe Line Under The Ocean – the cross-channel submarine petrol pipeline which took fuel from Great Britain to Normandy). Neither of these proposals was accepted, consequently the Admiralty informed ANCXF that the *Skiddaw* should be released to her owners.

Orders were issued on 18 April 1945 for her to sail from Antwerp at 13.30 on 22 April to The Downs, for onward routing to Portsmouth. However, bad weather delayed her departure for twenty-four hours and she arrived in Portsmouth harbour on 26 April.

Holland

The *Glen Usk* had been laid up at Portsmouth following her decommissioning in November 1944. Early in 1945 the Director of Sea Transport released her on charter to the Dutch Government. She made her way initially to Antwerp, it is believed in February 1945, and then to the East Scheldt. In some measure she then reverted to duties similar to her peacetime role in the repatriation of Dutch families, ferrying them between various ports on the river. She also assisted in the rehabilitation of ports and harbours by acting as a supply ship, carrying construction gangs and building materials. Among the many buildings damaged during the war was the Scheldt pilots' hostel and the *Glen Usk* provided accommodation for the pilots during the course of the building's reconstruction. The following article appeared in a Swansea newspaper on 9 July 1945:

Pilots Floating Hostel
Ilfracombe Boat's War Job in Dutch River

The PS Glen Usk, well known before the war to thousands of South Walians, now lies a mile from the sea in Holland.

Her decks, once crowded with excited, summer-clad holiday-makers, are almost empty; and where once were heard the musical tones of Welsh song and speech, there is now the slow, unhurried rhythm of the Dutch tongue. Instead of the familiar houseflag, she wears the Dutch tricolour.

The war, in which she played a worthy part, has not been unkind to her, and she bears no outward signs of damage. There have been alterations to her superstructure but her engines, now silent, still look just as they did when they thrilled hundreds of small boys who begged to be allowed to go below and watch them.

Now she does duty as a floating hostel for the pilots of the River Scheldt, and her captain is a lieutenant commander in the Royal Netherlands Navy. [...]

As she lies, made fast to a cobbled quayside, the old folk on fine evenings sit at the doors of their pleasant red brick houses opposite and watch her; a dozen shouting, beclogged children play around her. Some of the more daring cross the gangway and venture on to her deck until their voices rouse the duty officer to come out and 'shoo' them away.

In fact, exactly as happened to us − how many years ago is it? − in Swansea.

This particular turn of duty ended with the opening of the rebuilt pilots' hostel in September 1945.

HOME AGAIN

Weary and worn, impoverished but undaunted, and now triumphant, we had a moment that was sublime. We gave thanks to God for the noblest of all His blessings, the sense that we had done our duty.

During the concluding months of the conflict the surviving steamers of the White Funnel fleet were released from their wartime duties. The *Ravenswood*, which had remained laid up in the River Tamar since August 1944, was the first home, arriving at Bristol on the evening of Monday 9 April 1945. Spectators lined the Portway and cheered her upriver as she entered the Cumberland Basin. The local press reported:

An old friend passed through the 'front door' of her home once more after a fine record of war service. [...] She heralds the happier days of peace and pleasure cruises.

At the end of May 1945, as the Ministry of War Transport had promised in November 1942, the *Ravenswood* was offered to P&A Campbell for purchase; the price being the nominal sum of £1,000. The company accepted the offer and she rejoined the White Funnel fleet on completion of the sale on 2 August 1945.

Mr Keen wrote to Mr Allen:

The Ravenswood *is slowly coming back to life. The dining saloon, below the main deck, is being divided up into cabins for the officers; the officers' accommodation in this ship was always very poor; for instance, the two engineers shared one room. A small bar is being put into her top saloon, after the style of the old* Brighton Belle, *but the most noticeable alteration of all seems to be the new plated-in, concealed paddle boxes, built as an experiment. My hope is that the original type of box will find favour.*

The *Skiddaw* arrived from Portsmouth on Thursday 17 May, proudly flying her long, white paying-off pendant, and looking 'resplendent' in her dazzling camouflage paint. Her personnel had many tales to tell; perhaps the most unusual being that of a ceremony which took place aboard during the early months of the war when the child of one of her officers was baptised in her wardroom. The ship's bell, upturned and with the clapper removed, was used as a font!

HMS Ravenswood *arriving at Bristol from Plymouth on the evening of Monday 9 April 1945.* (Edwin Keen)

HMS Ravenswood *in the Bristol City Docks in April 1945.* (Edwin Keen)

Left and below: *Aboard HMS* Skiddaw *in the River Avon on her return to Bristol from Portsmouth on Thursday 17 May 1945.* (Chris Collard Collection)

HMS Skiddaw *passing Hotwells Landing Stage, Bristol, on Thursday 17 May 1945.* (Ken Jenkins Collection)

HMS Skiddaw *arriving in the Cumberland Basin on Thursday 17 May 1945.* (Chris Collard Collection)

HMS Skiddaw *arriving in the Cumberland Basin on Thursday 17 May 1945.* (Chris Collard Collection)

HMS Skiddaw *in the Cumberland Basin, Thursday 17 May 1945. Her white paying-off pendant can be seen flying from her foremast. This varied in length depending on the length of service of the vessel; the longer the service, the longer the pendant.* (Ernest Dumbleton)

Above and below: *HMS* Skiddaw *at the Railway Wharf in the Bristol City Docks on Monday 28 May 1945. She has not yet been de-comissioned, therefore she is still flying the White Ensign.* (Edwin Keen)

The condition of the *Skiddaw* is best described by quoting one of Mr Keen's letters:

> *She is in a very bad state and it is expected that her reconditioning will be a long and, for the Admiralty, costly job. [...]*
>
> *When I went below my heart sank; she seems to be a hopeless wreck, but I am told that the* Ravenswood *was very much worse. The Skiddaw's forward saloon was the only recognisable part; it had a double row of lockers along both sides, she must have had an enormous crew. Her shortened after saloon and dining saloon are divided up into numerous cabins for the officers and petty officers. The after square* [the space at the bottom of the after companionway from the promenade deck to the main deck between the engine room and the after saloon] *does not exist, still more rooms having been built there, with panelling from the former officers' cabins in the lower deck forward, now the magazine. The engine room was in total darkness and I could scarcely make out anything. There are miles of wiring all over the ship and queer little cubby holes with electrical devices, meaningless to me.*
>
> *Well, we have her back again and I shall be interested to see the transformation from a ghastly ruin running with cockroaches to the 'Queen of the Bristol Channel' [...]*

The *Glenmore*, having completed her duties for the RAF, was the next steamer to return. She was due to arrive from Antwerp on the evening of Sunday 24 June but, rather frustratingly for her crew and their waiting families, she ran very short of coal in the upper reaches of the Bristol Channel and had to put into Avonmouth Dock that evening to bunker, before arriving at Bristol on the following morning's high tide.

HMS Glenmore *making her way upriver from Avonmouth and Antwerp on the morning of Monday 25 June 1945.* (Ernest Dumbleton)

HMS Glenmore *making her way upriver from Avonmouth and Antwerp on the morning of Monday 25 June 1945.* (Ernest Dumbleton)

HMS Glenmore *about to enter the Cumberland Basin locks on Monday 25 June 1945.* (Ernest Dumbleton)

A view of the bridge of HMS Glenmore, *showing the anti-aircraft protection, as she passes through the Cumberland Basin locks on Monday 25 June 1945. Lt-Com. Shedden is just discernible at the telegraph on the port bridge wing.* (Ernest Dumbleton)

The Dutch Government's charter of the *Glen Usk* ended in the autumn of 1945. She was laid up at Antwerp from 9 to 29 September when she sailed for Southampton, arriving on the following day. She then sailed on 1 October and arrived in Bristol two days later.

Above: *HMS* Glen Usk *in the River Avon, returning to Bristol from Portsmouth, on the evening of Wednesday 3 October 1945.* (Chris Collard Collection)

Right: *HMS* Glen Usk *at Hotwells Landing Stage. Wednesday 3 October 1945.* (Chris Collard Collection)

ECHO OF BRISTOL
CHANNEL CRUISES

Lieut.-Commander
F. A. Smyth killed

Much sympathy will be felt in Swansea with Mr. Arthur E. Smyth, of Muldhu, Chambercombe Park, Ilfracombe. who in pre-war days was the Swansea representative of Messrs. P. and A. Campbell's white funnel fleet, at the death, by enemy action, of his son. Lieutenant-Commander Fredk. Arthur Smyth, R.N.R.

Lieut.-Commander Smyth will be remembered as the captain of the P.S. Waverley, one of the Campbell fleet, which carried thousands of holiday-makers on cruises in the Bristol Channel.

In the early days of the war. when serving on a mine-sweeper, his ship was one of the first to shoot down a German aircraft.

He assisted in the evacuation from Dunkirk, took an active part in D-Day operations, and was reported missing after five and a half years' strenuous service. Subsequent information indicates that he was killed on March 20.

Left: A report of the death, in 1945, of the former P&A Campbell master, Capt. Fred 'Ginger' Smyth.

Below: A newspaper report from the spring of 1945. The information it contains is somewhat inaccurate, but many years were to pass before the official records became available to the public.

WHAT CAMPBELLS' PLEASURE STEAMERS HAVE DONE DURING THE WAR

Five of the Eleven Will Not Return

By S. J. H., OUR SHIPPING CORRESPONDENT

Immediately after the declaration of war all eleven paddle-steamers of the P. and A. Campbell fleet were requisitioned, and in addition the Queen Empress—a turbine-engined twin-screw vessel building on the Clyde for the company—was taken over.

WHAT has happened to them? Well, all 11 paddle steamers were equipped for mine sweeping, and by the end of Sept. 1939 most of them (some bearing new names) set out to work until 1942 on the East Coast, between the North of Scotland and the Thames Estuary.

Britannia became Skiddaw; Cambria, Plinlimmon; Glen Gower, Glenmore; Waverley, Snaefell; and Empress Queen, Queen Eagle.

In 1940 seven of the fleet took part in the Dunkirk evacuation, and many thousands of men were ferried across the English Channel by them in numerous hazardous trips.

Of the seven, three—Brighton Queen, Devonia, and Brighton Belle—went down in a hail of bombs.

Escapes and Rescues

While all had amazing escapes, the experience of the Glen Gower (Glenmore) was unique, in that she survived. with the help of Snaefell (Waverley) a determined enemy attack In attempting to get as near to the beach as possible on one of her trips, Glenmore (Glen Gower) grounded. Snaefell (Waverley), with her complement of soldiers aboard went to the rescue and succeeded in towing her to deep water, both craft being under shell fire the whole of the time.

At one time Glenmore was the target of a shore battery, which scored only one hit. This "unlucky shot" (as one of the crew described it) penetrated the deck, leaving a gaping hole and killing 12 soldiers sleeping.

One of the narrowest escapes that befell Britannia (Skiddaw) occurred in 1940, when, in the course of big sweeps, a mine exploded close to her stern, shaking her badly; but she escaped structural damage.

Waverley Lost

Glenavon escaped disaster by a very narrow margin when Snaefell (Waverley) was sunk off the north-east coast in 1941.

The vessels were in company when the bomb which ended Snaefell's career exploded. Glenavon was so close that the concussion and blast shook her very badly, but the resulting damage was comparatively slight.

In 1942 the White Funnel vessels that had survived were transferred to new duties, and they have proved very successful as Ack-Ack ships, but Glenavon has been lost.

Thus five of the 11 ships of the fleet which set out from Bristol in 1939 will not return.

The *Ravenswood*, *Britannia* (ex-*Skiddaw*), *Glen Gower* (ex-*Glenmore*), and *Glen Usk* were taken in hand, both in the Underfall Yard and in Charles Hill & Son's dry dock and yards for refitting. Of the four ships, the condition of the *Glen Gower* was by far the worst necessitating, among a multitude of other tasks, the construction of a new bridge and the replacement of her promenade decking. The work was to preclude her return to service until 1947. The other three steamers, however, began service at intervals during the 1946 season; an extraordinary achievement considering the shortages of manpower and materials which prevailed at the time.

After the D-Day landings the personnel accommodated by the *Westward Ho* gradually left her and the ship had since remained at her moorings in the River Dart.

HMS Westward Ho *laid up in the River Dart in the autumn of 1945.* (Petty Officer Wilcox)

HMS Westward Ho *laid up in the River Dart in the autumn of 1945.* (Petty Officer Wilcox)

A letter to P&A Campbell from the Ministry of War Transport, dated 6 May 1946, states:

I am to confirm that the Ministry agrees to the retention, without payment by the owners, of the Admiralty fittings remaining on board the Westward Ho. *It is further agreed that the re-delivery of the vessel is to be regarded as having been effective on Thursday 2 May 1946, and that hire ceased from that date.*

Following discussions between Mr Banks and the Ministry of War Transport, a figure of £35,000 was agreed upon as compensation for her war service.

It was then necessary for P&A Campbell, at their own expense, to make arrangements for the *Westward Ho*'s return to Bristol.

The tug *Eastleigh* sailed from Avonmouth at 07.00 on Tuesday 14 May and arrived alongside her at 15.00 on the following day to tow her home. The two ships left Dartmouth at 05.00 on Thursday 16 May, cleared the River Dart at 06.30, and proceeded on the long, slow haul to Bristol. The memorandum book gives the details of their journey:

Friday 17 May 1946
02.30 Passed The Lizard. Fine weather.
11.50 Passed Pendeen Watch.
18.55 Passed Trevose Head.

Saturday 18 May 1946
01.50 Passed Hartland Point.
10.00 8 miles east of Ilfracombe.
18.00 Passed Barry.
20.00 Anchored in Walton Bay.

A story, of questionable authenticity, has been told of a particularly eerie incident experienced by the tug's crew during the voyage. Since taking up her duties as an accommodation ship at the beginning of 1944, the *Westward Ho*'s machinery had received no attention, consequently, her engine and paddle shafts had seized up. Her paddle wheels were jammed, and their immobility caused a considerable drag on the tow. In the darkness of the still, calm night, while in the vicinity of The Lizard, the crew of the tug were astonished to hear the paddles of the deserted ship slowly turning – a phenomenon to form the basis of many a spine-chilling ghost story no doubt – but reality admits of a much more prosaic explanation. The continuous pressure of water against the paddle floats had set them in motion!

The *Westward Ho* arrived at Bristol at 10.15 on the morning of Sunday 19 May 1946 and was moored at the Underfall Yard. A survey indicated that the years of neglect had taken serious toll, and this, in addition to her condemned boiler, precluded her return to civilian service. She was accordingly advertised for sale and was purchased, for £800, in July 1946 by the Newport shipbreakers, John Cashmore & Son Ltd.

On the evening of Wednesday 31 July she began her last journey, in tow of the tugs *John King* and *Volunteer*, when at 20.00 she left the Underfall Yard and was manoeuvred into the Cumberland Basin. At 21.00 she left the locks and entered the River Avon, where, an hour later a somewhat poignant encounter was experienced when the *Glen Usk* passed her on her return from Ilfracombe with a full complement of passengers. One of those passengers was Mr Edwin Keen, who, in conversation with the author in the mid-1960s, commented, 'What a sad sight she presented. Even after all these years the recollection of it still brings a lump to my throat.' The *Westward Ho* was berthed at Cashmore's Yard, on the west bank of the River Usk, on the following morning.

The Westward Ho *in the River Avon, returning to Bristol from Dartmouth. Sunday 19 May 1946.* (Ernest Dumbleton)

Above and below: *The* Westward Ho *in the River Avon, returning to Bristol from Dartmouth. Sunday 19 May 1946.* (Ernest Dumbleton)

Above and below: *The* Westward Ho *at the Underfall Yard, Bristol. Tuesday 21 May 1946.* (Edwin Keen)

The Westward Ho *at the Underfall Yard, Bristol. June 1946.* (W.J. Kerswell)

The Westward Ho *being towed from the Underfall Yard on her final journey, Wednesday 31 July 1946.* (Chris Collard Collection)

Above: *The* Westward Ho *entering the Cumberland Basin on the evening of Wednesday 31 July 1946.* (Ken Jenkins Collection)

Right: *A report of the* Westward Ho*'s final journey, from the 'South Wales Argus' on Thursday 1 August 1946.*

"Westward Ho's" Last Trip

"Westward Ho," a P. and A. Campbell pleasure steamer which carried thousands of Monmouthshire people to Bristol Channel resorts, and performed gallant services during the War, is to be broken up at the Newport yard of John Cashmore, Limited.

The steamer, built in 1894, is 225ft. in length and 26ft. in beam. She is to be broken up because of her age and damage suffered during the War.

When war started, "Westward Ho" was "called up" as a minesweeper in the Channel. The steamer also took part in evacuation of British troops from Dunkirk. During later stages of the War, she had a quieter career, as a Royal Navy depot ship at Dartmouth.

"Westward Ho" will make her last trip up the River Usk at eight o'clock on Thursday morning. The vessel will be broken up in sight of the landing stage at which holiday crowds boarded her in her heyday.

The Westward Ho *arriving at John Cashmore's Yard, Newport, on the morning of Thursday 1 August 1946.* (Lionel Vaughan Collection)

A fate similar to that of the *Westward Ho* befell her sister ship, the *Cambria* (ex-*Plinlimmon*), lying in the London Dock East. In addition to the ravages of neglect she had been further damaged by a fire which had broken out on board early in August 1946. The Ministry of War Transport offered P&A Campbell £35,000 in settlement of its liabilities for her, then offered to buy her for £300 as she lay, less certain items of equipment to be specified by the company, and to dispose of her for scrap; offers which the company accepted on 15 August. Accordingly, during the following winter she was broken up by Thomas Ward & Co. without returning to her home port. She was towed to their yard at Grays, Essex, where, as Mr Allen wrote, 'She joined dozens of sloops, destroyers and similar craft awaiting disposal; the assembled fleet presenting a very dismal picture.'

On 9 December 1946 she was moved to the breaking-up berth where the cutters began their work. She had been there only a few hours when, for the second time, she caught fire. The cutters had ceased work for tea and by the time they returned she was well ablaze. Firemen were called who stated that sparks from their blow-torches were probably responsible and that oil in the engine room fed the flames. It was necessary for them to cut holes in the sides of her hull to let the rising tide flow in to put the fire out!

On a foggy winter morning, the barely discernible Cambria *(ex-*Plinlimmon*) (nearer the camera) lies alongside half of a destroyer in the London Dock East, 16 November 1946. Both vessels were awaiting transfer to the breakers' yard.* (H.A. Allen)

The Cambria *on fire at the yard of Thomas Ward & Co. at Grays, Essex, on Tuesday 9 December 1946.* (Chris Collard Collection)

Left and below: *The* Cambria *on fire at the yard of Thomas Ward & Co. at Grays, Essex, on Tuesday 9 December 1946.* (Chris Collard Collection)

While the company was immersed in paddle steamer matters, the turbine steamer, *Empress Queen*, continued her services between Stranraer and Larne. She was under the command of Capt. Jack George, the Commodore of the White Funnel fleet, and although the vessel operated under the management of the General Steam Navigation Co., on behalf of the Ministry of War Transport, Capt. George kept her owners fully informed of her activities. As an example an entry from the memorandum book of 1946 is quoted:

> *Capt. George writes – '18 January – Empress Queen damaged upper portion of stock of bow rudder and steering gear above deck level after leaving Stranraer and proceeding down Loch Ryan. Apparently caused through neglecting to see that rudder was properly secured on the previous night. Messrs Kane of Larne have job in hand. [...]*
>
> *Between beginning on the route on 7 January 1944 and 31 December 1945, 534,290 service personnel have been carried. Civilian passengers have also been carried when on the mail run, relieving Royal Daffodil. [...]*
>
> *On a recent day – caught in bad weather on the way over and had to turn back to Stranraer. Great difficulty in steering – had to assist by reducing speed of one engine. Captain of Princess Maud said it was worst crossing he had ever made.'*

She made her last round trip on Saturday 5 October 1946, having carried over 600,000 Allied Army, Navy and Air Force personnel since she had been placed on the service.

The Empress Queen *leaving Stranraer, 1946.* (Ken Jenkins Collection)

The Empress Queen *leaving Stranraer, 1946.* (Donald Anderson Collection)

On Tuesday 8 October the *Empress Queen* left Stranraer at 06.00 and at 10.15 arrived at Troon, where her builders, the Ailsa Shipbuilding Co. were to undertake her refit. The additional cost to P&A Campbell of completing and furnishing the vessel for civilian service amounted to £19,256, of which the Ministry of War Transport agreed to pay £7,000. As the Ailsa Co. had suggested in 1940, on completion of her refit she ran further trials on the measured mile off the Isle of Arran. These took place on Monday 16 June 1947 and were entirely satisfactory. Her delivery voyage began on the following day and ended when she arrived at Bristol on the evening of Wednesday 18 June 1947, over seven years after her launch.

As the war had drawn to its close, the management of P&A Campbell had considered the future of its seriously depleted fleet. The board had sanctioned the building of a new paddle steamer in July 1944, but the Director of Merchant Shipping had refused the necessary license owing to more pressing demands for war needs.

On 23 January 1945 Mr Banks reported that a quote had been received from Charles Hill & Sons Ltd for a steamer '245 feet in length, with a speed of 17 knots (loaded) at a cost of £115,000'. The quote was accepted by the board but it was not until the following month that the license for construction was forthcoming. The contract for the new steamer was signed on Wednesday 4 April 1945.

What lay ahead for P&A Campbell as the company, for the second time in its history, picked up the threads of conflict and re-formed its decimated fleet? A new paddle steamer had been ordered, and rumours were rife that more were to follow, but few could envisage the course which history was to take. Another heroic struggle was destined to take place in the years to come, this time against the harsh and unyielding economics of a changing world. But then, in the euphoria of peace after the dark days of war, feelings of optimism were foremost.

The company's minute book effectively closed its war chapter and looked forward to the future. The final entry of the final board meeting of 1945 states:

It was proposed, discussed and agreed that the new steamer be named Bristol Queen.

RETURNING TO SERVICE

Operations in 1946 were handicapped by the total destruction of Minehead pier, by the tardy de-requisitioning of Weston-super-Mare pier, and by doubts as to the safety of Clevedon pier. [...] Nevertheless, the ships ran packed to the limit with passengers eager to sample the benefits of fresh sea air, and to initiate a new generation of children into its delights.

Grahame Farr
West Country Passenger Steamers

As the Second World War continued and the Royal Navy's purpose-built vessels increased in number, so the hired paddle steamers were consigned to more modest roles; their services no longer so desperately required. But they had answered the call when they had been most needed; defying the perils of minesweeping in the North Sea, bringing home the troops of the ill-fated British Expeditionary Force, and protecting the cargo ships bringing vital supplies to British shores.

The censorship of news restricted the reporting of even the major operations of the conflict; consequently, the activities of the thousands of minor war vessels were largely unknown to the general public. They knew little of the dangers that the summer excursion vessels and their gallant personnel had faced, nor how they had faced those dangers with a zeal as great as that of their more exalted consorts.

In the autumn of 1939 the eleven paddle steamers of the White Funnel fleet proudly stood in Bristol's floating harbour. In the autumn of 1945 there were only four – four forlorn ships in the heart of a city reeling in the aftermath of five catastrophic years.

It was, however, a time for reconstruction, refurbishment and renovation, and this final series of photographs follows the course of preparation of the surviving steamers for the resumption of their sailings, culminating in their first days of post-war Bristol Channel service.

The White Funnel fleet was, once again, in business!

The Britannia *and* Glen Gower *at the Underfall Yard in June 1945.* (W.J. Kerswell)

The Britannia *alongside the* Glen Gower *at the Underfall Yard, June 1945.* (Ken Jenkins Collection)

The Glen Gower *at the Underfall Yard. Sunday 1 July 1945.* (Edwin Keen)

The Ravenswood *in the Merchant's Dock, Bristol, with her refit under way. Sunday 30 September 1945.*
(Edwin Keen)

An article which appeared in a Bristol newspaper on Friday 18 May 1945. The prospect of the resumption of sailings in July of that year was rather over optimistic considering the post-war shortage of materials and manpower.

RAVENSWOOD GETTING READY

Trips in July?

AFTER an absence of over five years the familiar house-flag and ship decoration of the White Funnel fleet will probably be seen in the Bristol Channel early in July.

Ravenswood, the first of the fleet to return from war service, is again under the control of Messrs. P. and A. Campbell, Ltd.

She has emerged from drydock, and just above her present water-line can be seen the foundation of the well-known colour scheme that in peace-time adorns all the ships of the fleet.

Transformation above and below decks is proceeding rapidly, and, so far as Messrs. Campbell are concerned, Ravenswood will be ready to take her former place on the Weston-Cardiff ferry service in the first or second week of July. The definite re-opening of the service, however, is contingent upon certain circumstances over which Messrs. Campbell have no control.

Principals of the firm are hopeful that the difficulties will be removed by the time Ravenswood is ready.

The White Funnel Fleet's first post-war paddle steamer, Bristol Queen, *being launched at Charles Hill's Yard on Thursday 4 April 1946. Outside the yard is the* Britannia, *undergoing her post-war refit.* (Edwin Keen)

The Britannia *and* Glen Usk *at the Underfall Yard on Sunday 21 October 1945.* (Edwin Keen)

P. & A. CAMPBELL LIMITED

Directors :

GEORGE HERBERT BOUCHER.   WILLIAM JAMES BANKS.
WILLIAM GERARD BANKS.
ROBERT JAMES TURNER CAMPBELL.
JOSEPH WILLIAM JOHN JENKINS.

DIRECTORS' REPORT

TO BE SUBMITTED

At the FIFTY-FOURTH ORDINARY GENERAL MEETING to be held at the GRAND HOTEL, BRISTOL, on FRIDAY, MAY 10th, 1946, at 12 noon.

The Directors herewith present the Balance Sheet for the year ending 31st December, 1945.

After payment of the Dividend on the Preference Shares at the rate of Six per cent. per annum (*less* Income Tax), there remains a balance of £16,383 6s. 10d. which the Directors recommend should be dealt with as follows :—

To Dividend on the Ordinary Shares of Six per cent. (*less* Income Tax)	...	...	...	...	...	6,600	0 0
„ Taxation Reserve	...	...	...	...	...	5,500	0 0
„ General Reserve	...	...	...	...	...	2,000	0 0

leaving £2,283 6s. 10d. to be carried forward to the next account.

During the year the Directors placed an order with Messrs. Charles Hill & Sons Ltd., Bristol, for the construction of a new Paddle Steamer for service in the Bristol Channel. This Steamer, named " Bristol Queen," has now been launched, and should be in commission by July of this year.

The Cross Channel Steamer " Empress Queen " and the P.S. " Cambria " are still on charter to the Government. The P.S. " Britannia," " Glen Gower " and " Glen Usk," having been released, are being reconditioned and will resume sailings in the Bristol Channel as they become available, while the P.S. " Westward Ho " has now finished service with the Admiralty and will shortly be derequisitioned. Sailings in the Bristol Channel by the P.S. " Ravenswood " have already commenced. It is regretted that the Company lost five vessels while on active service.

Mr. George Herbert Boucher retires by rotation, and being eligible, offers himself for re-election.

Messrs. Ham, Jackson & Brown, the Auditors, also retire, and offer themselves for re-election.

G. H. BOUCHER, *Chairman.*

W. J. BANKS, *Managing Director.*

J. W. J. JENKINS, *Secretary.*

May 1st, 1946.

Part of the directors' report submitted to the Annual General Meeting of 1946.

The Glen Usk *outside Hill's Yard on Friday 10 May 1946. On the extreme left, the* Glen Gower *can be seen in dry dock and, on the right, the* Bristol Queen *can be seen fitting out.* (Edwin Keen)

The Britannia *nearing completion of refitting at Hill's Yard. Friday 10 May 1946.* (Edwin Keen)

The Glen Gower *outside Hill's Yard in July 1946. Ahead of her is the* Glen Usk, *her refit nearly complete.* (Donald Anderson Collection)

The Glen Gower *at the Mardyke Wharf.* (H.G. Owen Collection)

Aboard the Glen Gower *on Sunday 28 July 1946. Her new bridge is under construction and her promenade decking is being renewed.* (H.G. Owen)

The Glen Gower *outside Hill's Yard on Sunday 28 July 1946.* (H.G. Owen)

Work has just started on the Empress Queen's *post-war refit at the Ailsa Shipbuilding Co.'s Yard at Troon, in November 1946.* (Graham E. Langmuir)

The Empress Queen *undergoing her post-war refit, in the spring of 1947.* (Graham E. Langmuir)

The Empress Queen *nearing completion of her post-war refit, May 1947.* (H.G. Owen Collection)

The Empress Queen *on trials in the Firth of Clyde, Monday 16 June 1947.* (W. Ralston)

Tuesday. 17th June. 1947. At Troon.

9000:- Crew take over vessel from Ailsa Shipbuilding Company after refit.

8AM. Fresh W'ly breeze overcast & cloudy.

Noon:- Fresh breeze cloudy & occ showers.

2PM. All tanks & bilges sounded Draught. $\begin{cases} F & 7'\ 07" \\ A & 7'\ 11" \\ M & 7'\ 09" \end{cases}$

4PM. Fresh NW wind overcast & cloudy.
4.55. Cast off moorings & proceeded stern first. 5PM. Full speed
5.15. Abm. Lady Isle. Course SW½W.
6.35 Abm Ailsa Craig 4p Co. SxW¾W. log set.
7.30 Abm Corswell point. 7.58 Black Head abm. log 21.
9.30 M. South Rock Lt. Vsl. abm log 45.

1200 Mid:- Fresh - Strong N.W breeze overcast & cloudy.

J. S. George
Master.

Above and opposite: *The log of the* Empress Queen's *journey from Troon to Bristol.*

Wed.   18th June 1947.
Seoan   towards   Bristol.

4 AM.	Strong breeze overcast & cloudy. Course S×W¾W.
6.12 AM.	Abm South Bishop Rock dist 1' log 184 a/c 155° mag.
6.42 AM.	a/c 165° mag., 7AM Abm Skokholm light a/c 130° mag.
8 AM.	Fresh wly wind cloudy.
8.02	St Govens Head abm a/c 124° mag.
8.20 AM.	Speed reduced to coincide with E.T.A
10 AM.	a/c to 107° (mag)
11.00	Abm Scarweather lt. Vsl. log 258.
11.●	Foreland abeam dist 6½'
Noon	log 267. Course. 107° mag.
12.36.	Abeam Nash point
1 PM.	a/c 090° Mag.
1.45 PM	Let go port ♄ in Barry Roads. Moderate/slight breeze fine clear weather.
5.50 PM.	Stand by Engines, 6.10 ♄ aweigh Course E⅓S.
6.25	Sully Island a/Co E⅓N, 6.27 West Cardiff buoy.
6.32	Monkstone Co ExN. 6.39. Hope buoy ExN½N.
6.45	N.W. Elbow. 6.52 N. Elbow E¾S. 7.18 Firefly buoy.
7.24	Avon light house. 7.30 Tugs.{ F. John Kry A. Volunteer. fast.
7.50	Sea Mills 8.07 Locks. 8.35 Cumberland Basin
	Securely moored fore & aft. Star side to
●	Day ends light S'thly wind overcast & cloudy

Distance 368'

J.S. George
Master.

The Ravenswood *leaving Bristol on the first post-war trip, an afternoon cruise to off Clevedon, on Saturday 13 April 1946. (Bristol Evening Post)*

CAMPBELL'S SAILINGS

for

1946

Easter Holidays

by

P.S. Ravenswood

From BRISTOL (Hotwells Landing Stage)

(Weather and circumstances permitting)

SATURDAY, APRIL 13th

3.30 p.m. Afternoon CRUISE DOWN CHANNEL passing Walton Bay and to off Clevedon, back about 6.0 p.m. **Fare 3/6.**
6.30 p.m. Single Trip to CARDIFF.

SUNDAY, APRIL 14th

6.0 p.m. Evening CRUISE DOWN CHANNEL to Walton Bay, back about 8.0 p.m. **Fare 3/6.**
8.15 p.m. Single Trip to CARDIFF.
　　NOTE.—A Steamer leaves Cardiff 3.45 p.m. for Bristol.

MONDAY, APRIL 15th

6.30 p.m. Evening CRUISE DOWN CHANNEL to Walton Bay, back about 8.30 p.m. **Fare 3/6.**
8.45 p.m. Single Trip to PENARTH and CARDIFF.
　　NOTE.—A Steamer leaves Cardiff 4.15 p.m., Penarth 4.25 p.m. for Bristol.

TUESDAY, APRIL 16th

　　NO SAILINGS THIS DAY.

WEDNESDAY, APRIL 17th

9.45 a.m. Day Trip to PENARTH and CARDIFF. Leave Cardiff 5.15 p.m., Penarth 5.25 p.m., due Bristol about 7.10 p.m.
7.20 p.m. Evening CRUISE DOWN CHANNEL to Walton Bay, back about 9.20 p.m. **Fare 3/6.**
9.30 p.m. Single Trip to PENARTH and CARDIFF.
　　NOTE.—A Steamer leaves Cardiff 7.35 a.m., Penarth 7.45 a.m. for Bristol.

THURSDAY, APRIL 18th

　　NO SAILINGS THIS DAY.

GOOD FRIDAY, APRIL 19th

10.45 a.m. Day Trip to CARDIFF, PENARTH and BARRY PIER. Leave Barry Pier 5.15 p.m., Penarth 5.35 p.m., Cardiff 6.0 p.m., due Bristol about 7.50 p.m.
8.30 p.m. Single Trip to PENARTH and CARDIFF.
　　NOTE.—A Steamer leaves Cardiff 8.20 a.m., Penarth 8.30 a.m. for Bristol.

SATURDAY, APRIL 20th

11.0 a.m. Day Trip to CARDIFF, PENARTH and BARRY PIER. Leave Barry Pier 5.45 p.m., Penarth 6.5 p.m., Cardiff 6.30 p.m., due Bristol about 8.30 p.m.
8.45 p.m. Single Trip to PENARTH and CARDIFF.
　　NOTE.—A Steamer leaves Cardiff 8.45 a.m., Penarth 8.55 a.m. for Bristol.

EASTER SUNDAY, APRIL 21st

11.30 a.m. Day Trip to BARRY PIER. Leave Barry Pier 5.45 p.m., due Bristol about 8.15 p.m.
8.20 p.m. Single Trip to NEWPORT. **Fare 5/6.**
　　NOTE.—A Steamer leaves Newport 9.0 a.m. for Bristol.

EASTER MONDAY, APRIL 22nd

10.20 a.m. Day Trip to PENARTH and CARDIFF. Leave Cardiff 6.45 p.m., Penarth 6.55 p.m., due Bristol about 8.50 p.m.
9.10 p.m. Single Trip to PENARTH and CARDIFF
　　NOTE.—A Steamer leaves Cardiff 8.0 a.m., Penarth 8.10 a.m. for Bristol.

EASTER TUESDAY, April 23rd

12.30 p.m. Afternoon Trip to CARDIFF, PENARTH and BARRY PIER. Leave Barry Pier 6.30 p.m., Penarth 6.50 p.m., Cardiff 7.15 p.m., due Bristol about 9.15 p.m.
9.30 p.m. Single Trip to PENARTH and CARDIFF.
　　NOTE.—A Steamer leaves Cardiff 10.0 a.m., Penarth 10.10 a.m. for Bristol.

The timetable for the first post-war sailings from Bristol.

The Britannia *in the Avon on her first post-war trip, from Bristol to Clevedon, Cardiff and Ilfracombe. Saturday 1 June 1946.* (H.G. Owen Collection)

The Glen Usk *in the Cumberland Basin on the afternoon of Wednesday 24 July 1946. She is about to leave for Cardiff and to begin her post-war sailings.* (Edwin Keen)

The Empress Queen *leaving Swansea on her first passenger carrying sailing for P&A Campbell – a cruise around the Scarweather Lightvessel – on the evening of Friday 27 June 1947. (*H.G. Owen*)*

The Glen Gower began her post-war sailings on the South Coast on Wednesday 21 May 1947, but changed places with the Empress Queen *on the Swansea station owing to the unsuitability of the latter for Bristol Channel running. The Glen Gower is seen here returning from a day trip to Ilfracombe on her first day in post-war Bristol Channel service – Tuesday 15 July 1947.* (H.G. Owen)

INDEX

Names in *italics* are those of ships. Numbers in **bold** refer to illustrations.